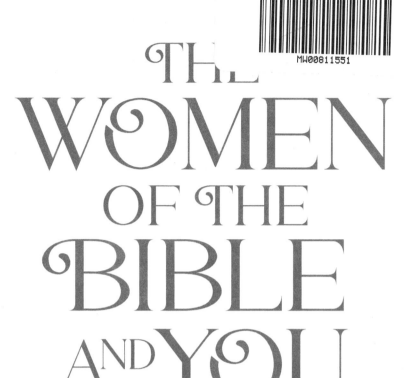

THE WOMEN OF THE BIBLE AND YOU

A WEEKLY DEVOTIONAL

ARIONNE YVETTE WILLIAMS

ROCKRIDGE
PRESS

Interior & Cover Designer: Lisa Schreiber
Art Producer: Tom Hood
Editor: Lauren O'Neal
Production Editor: Nora Milman

Author photograph courtesy of Arionne Yvette Williams

ISBN: Print 978-1-64152-811-5 | eBook 978-1-64152-812-2

R0

To William, my sweetheart,
who encouraged me every step
of the way *throughout this project.*
I will forever be grateful!

To the many women
and girls who've inspired
the words and stories shared here.
Thank you!

CONTENTS

INTRODUCTION

Hello there! I'm thrilled you've picked up this book, and I'm so excited to share this journey with you. My name is Arionne, and though I wear many hats—fiancée, minister, college chaplain, daughter, sister, friend, confidante, and many more—at the end of the day, I consider myself a girl's girl. I love women, and I have always been passionate about women's empowerment and celebrating and telling women's stories.

Women's stories are very present in the Bible and useful in helping us understand the history of Israel and the larger narrative of reconciling all people to God through Christ. But those stories are often overlooked. When I noticed this years ago, I made a personal commitment to preaching, teaching, and writing about the women of the Bible, named and unnamed. With this book, I aim to explore some of the beautiful devotional content readily available in their stories.

While we're often left wanting more detail on these women beyond what's in the text, there is so much to gain from what is there and what is just beneath and behind the text. We can see how the women of the Bible overcame their challenges and perhaps be inspired to overcome our own. We can see the power in the telling of their stories and maybe find the courage to tell our own. We can learn about some of the untold, rarely discussed women and all they have to say to us in contemporary times. It's not easy being a woman now, and it wasn't any easier then. These women were often up against systems of oppression and societies that overlooked them. But they still made their marks on the world, and so can we.

In exploring these women's stories, I tried to tell their truths and provide relevant background information that helps give meaning and shape to their stories. I'm here not to judge them but to allow them to be central to their own story. It's important to recognize that some of these women appear in stories in which they are not the heroine or central figure. Often, they're only mentioned in passing in service of some other story. But I contend that even in those instances, they have something powerful and important to say, and we should listen.

As you engage with each woman's story, know that you are entering her world, with all the different cultural assumptions and conventions that shaped her reality. Each story will show you more about that world and help you understand and appreciate these women's actions. I encourage you to read and enjoy what these women have to say and allow their stories to inspire you for faithful living.

Happy reading!

HOW TO USE THIS BOOK

Studying scripture can be overwhelming just because of the sheer volume of it; it can be difficult to know where to start. This book is organized in a way to help alleviate that. It includes 52 devotions, one for each week of the year. Each devotion features scripture and commentary about a woman of the Bible or a topic important to contemporary women seeking to live faithfully in their relationship with God in Christ. By the end, you'll have learned about many different women—standout characters of the Bible like Eve, Sarah, Esther, Ruth, and Mary, as well as some lesser-known women like Anna the prophetess and the Syrophoenician woman.

I realize that reading this book is a real commitment of your time and energy, but there is so much to learn from the women of the Bible. I encourage you to take seriously the journey you're making, open yourself to the possibilities for learning, and commit yourself to the experience. Take your time working through it. Sit in study and reflection with the book for at least a half hour each week. You can do this alone, with another person, or even with a group of friends or a small group at church.

INDIVIDUAL STUDY

If you decide to read this book on your own, think of it as a key part of your devotional time with God each day. You can begin each week with a prayer, inviting God to guide you through this experience, and then read that week's devotion. Write down any questions that come up as you read. Then spend a day or two thinking, praying, and reflecting on what you've read. If you don't get any immediate answers, that's okay. Just sit with your questions.

Share your experience with God in prayer. Keep a notebook or folder that includes all your thoughts, questions, and insights. Though the book has some prompts for prayer, reflection, and journaling, don't feel limited by those alone. Feel free to journal on each entry if you'd like.

I also encourage you to share your thoughts with a trusted friend or loved one. This can be someone who's reading with you or not. Either way, I recommend asking them to be a true conversation partner, *not* to enter "teaching" mode or tell you how you should think or feel about your experience. Instead, they should listen and share with you what they've heard you say and how they've watched your journey along the way.

Once you have completed this book after a year of reading, find a way to celebrate it with a special dinner or other treat for yourself! Write down major learnings and experiences you've had in reading the book. Share your thoughts with loved ones.

GROUP STUDY

Studying in a small group (8 to 10 people, preferably) is an awesome way to experience this book. Since a year of weekly meetings might be hard to do, I suggest meeting for a few months instead. If you meet for 13 weeks, you could cover four devotions per week—or just select 13 devotions to read as a group and read the other 39 on your own. However you choose to do it, allow the reading to shape your discussion each week. Have everyone read on their own beforehand, writing down any questions, thoughts, feelings, and insights that come up. Then each person should be prepared to share their thoughts in the meeting. Here are some good questions to help guide the discussion:

- What did you think or feel about this woman/topic?

- How did you see yourself in the story? Can you identify with a particular person? Why or why not?

- How do you connect to the lesson offered in the devotion?

- What lingering questions do you have?

And here are some best practices for group study:

- Meet weekly in the context of small group study for as long a period as your group chooses. (One year of weekly meetings might be hard to do.) If getting together in person each week is hard, feel free to use technology and meet online.

- Plan for about 60 to 90 minutes per session.

- Pray together each week for open listening, learning, and growth.

- Keep sessions confidential. They should be a safe space for everyone to share how they really feel, knowing that it won't be shared elsewhere. (This includes no sharing with spouses without express permission!)

- When sharing your opinions, speak about your own journey and how you are connecting to the text. Use "I" statements.

- Don't judge. Simply listen and support. Fight the urge to "fix" each other. God is the fixer for us all.

- Try not to debate. This is about deepening your devotional life with God, not about being right or wrong on a theological matter. People within a group might have different viewpoints on a story or topic. That's okay! Embrace that diversity.

- Have fun! Laughter is a good thing. No need to be overly serious. Connect with those in your group. Enjoy the experience.

- Once you've finished, plan a party or gathering to allow your group to celebrate the experience! Working through something like this is a major accomplishment!

FURTHER STUDY

At the end of the year, you can start over and do it again or just pick this book up whenever you want to revisit it. It can be so interesting to see what new insights appear for you after some time has passed. You can also consult the resources listed at the end of the book for more in-depth information on the women I've profiled (and some I haven't).

PART I

EVE: GOD'S GRACE MADE REAL

The man Adam knew his wife Eve
intimately. She became pregnant and
gave birth to Cain, and said, "I have
given life to a man with the Lord's help."
∾ GENESIS 4:1 (CEB)

Eve, like most women you and I know, took on many roles—
wife, companion, mother. But if you peek just below the surface of her story, someone much more layered emerges: a
survivor, pioneer, and creator of culture. Eve was a leader
who pushed the bounds of life further than perhaps even she
could have imagined. We've all heard about her fateful choice
to eat the forbidden fruit, as told in Genesis 3, but what happened in the aftermath of that life-altering moment? What
did she learn about herself, about God, about grace, about
moving on and finding new purpose?

When we encounter Eve in Genesis 4:1, her life has already
taken quite a few blows. In an earlier season, she had lived

with her husband in a luscious garden teeming with biological diversity, where God took strolls to catch the afternoon breeze. It was a dream. But one moment had undone it all. God had banished them from their picturesque home, forcing them to work the land and her to suffer labor pains. Perhaps even worse, suddenly a hierarchy existed between Eve and her husband. It was a lot, but it was her new reality.

Maybe you've had a taste of something like Eve's new reality. Perhaps you lost a job, a friendship, or a marriage, and your life changed drastically. What you had or hoped for was suddenly far from reach, and you had no choice but to accept life as it was now, devoid of all the beauty and promise you once experienced. Maybe the vibrant, confident, purpose-driven person you once were shifted, and your insecurities, guilt, and shame emerged. Maybe the weight of it paralyzed you, and you had no idea how to get back to who you were and go after the life you wanted.

For me, that event was a call from a nurse, confirming my terrifying suspicion that I had contracted a sexually transmitted infection (STI). Here I was, a youth minister—called, anointed, speaking, teaching, preaching—and apparently walking around with an STI. It was curable, but my shame over where I was and how I had gotten there didn't feel curable at all. It was the lowest I had ever felt. How could I look at those teenagers, whom I was called to serve, and encourage them to pursue a relationship with God when I felt like such a failure in my own faith?

This is where Eve is so instructive. She shows us that survival is possible, that there is life on the other side of disaster, and that we are much more than our painful moments. She went through the worst of the worst and somehow managed to keep evolving. Genesis 4:1 shows her expression of joy and praise for what she and God were able to do *together*. For the first time, a woman had given birth, and she was blown away that she had done it. It didn't matter what had happened before. She was looking at this child she and Adam had created, deeply grateful God empowered her to bring forth life.

Therein lies the most powerful part of Eve's life lesson. She lost many things in that garden, but she didn't lose God. God had not given up on her. Though the narrative shows that God punished both her and Adam, banishing them from paradise, God walked out of the garden, too, and journeyed *with them* into this new life. The new reality was harsher than what they'd known, but they still had God.

No matter what life throws at you or how you may be judging yourself, hang on to your faith, knowing that God walks with you through it all. God is never intimidated by the lows of your story but gets right in there and finds a way to bring new life out of destruction and perceived failure. I had an STI. So what? Since then, I've been ordained an elder in my church, written a book, landed my dream job, found my dream love, and grown my love for myself. There is more glory and evolution ahead for you because God is with you and refuses to leave you, no matter what mistakes you make. Don't live in your past; God doesn't. Walk in the power of God's grace toward what promises and joy lie ahead for you.

WEEK 2

WHEN YOU KNOW WHO YOU ARE

Then the Lord God said, "It is not good
that the man should be alone; I will
make him a helper as his partner."
∽ GENESIS 2:18

Over the course of time, much ado has been made about this word "helper" that we find in Genesis 2:18 when God creates Adam and Eve. We often hear both men and women claiming that women were created for the sole purpose of helping men, but is this actually what God had in mind? What does this verse mean? How is it helpful for us? What does this verse reveal about what God wants for us? Whether you are conservative or progressive, there is much power packed in this passage for us all.

The Hebrew word translated into English as "helpmeet" or "helper" is *ezer*. Elsewhere in the Bible, it's used only to describe God's character, power, and ability to deliver aid and support. One famous place it's used is in Psalm 121:1–2: "I lift

4

up my eyes to the hills—from where will my help come? My help comes from the Lord, who made heaven and earth." The word for "help" in both instances is *ezer*.

Help, then, is certainly not the same as we often understand it in Western culture. When we hear "help," we often think of it as "*the* help," someone who's submissive or subservient. But *ezer* doesn't mean that in the Bible. So in Genesis, describing Eve as "helper" or "helpmeet" means she's powerfully resourceful, bringing Adam what he could never have had on his own. Her abilities are compared to God's. Is she divine? No. But her very presence transforms Adam's possibilities. And she can only do and be those things because of all the layers of awesomeness that God has placed in her, separate from Adam. She is her own person, with her own strength, personality, agency, and purpose. He is blessed once she shows up in his life.

What does this mean for you? In brief, sis, you are amazing. You're a well of wonder overflowing right where you stand. You were created in God's image, so you are certainly not beneath anybody, not at work, at home, or at school. You are capable, smart, insightful, strong, loyal, and beautiful inside and out. The sooner you realize this, the sooner you can live this truth. Always be aware of what you bring to the table. Nurture your spirit and soul, and make manifest this divinely crafted power of support, love, and wisdom you were always intended to be.

Please turn to the next page for a GUIDED REFLECTION. ⫸→

GUIDED REFLECTION

Is this understanding of the word "helper" different than how you've understood it before? Can you embrace it? What does it feel like to think of yourself as having divine-like abilities? How does this connect to the idea that you were created in God's image?

WEEK 3

LESS MONEY, MORE PROBLEMS

And Ruth the Moabite said to Naomi,
"Let me go to the field and glean
among the ears of grain, behind
someone in whose sight I may
find favor." She said to her, "Go, my
daughter." So she went. She came and
gleaned in the field behind the reapers.
∽ RUTH 2:2–3

In the book of Ruth, Naomi and her two daughters-in-law,
Ruth and Orpah, are part of a beautifully diverse family,
living in Ruth and Orpah's home country, Moab. But then
the men of the family die, leaving Naomi without sons and
all three women without husbands. Determined to support
Naomi, Orpah and Ruth want to accompany her back to her
hometown of Bethlehem. But Naomi demands that they go
back; she sees no way she can help them and figures they'll
fare better in Moab. Orpah concedes and tearfully returns,

7

but Ruth famously refuses. She has made up her mind that if she must find a new life, it will not be in Moab with her own people. It will be in Bethlehem with Naomi and hers.

One problem: They have no money, no men, and no plan. This was no small thing for women in their world. In their culture, men held the power and family inheritance was patrilineal (Ruth 4:1–6). If a woman had no connection to a man, she had no real economic stability. Ruth and Naomi's loss wasn't merely emotional—it also left them poor and very vulnerable.

At its core, this story is about the human spirit's desire to triumph over tragedy. When we encounter Ruth in chapter 2, she's plotting a comeback with no budget and no husband, fueled by a determination to make this new life work *and* by a deep devotion to Naomi. This is a classic story of a woman doing what she had to do. She had to make a way for herself and her new family, even if she had to scrimp and save for the rest of her life. So she headed to a field owned by a man she had never met, to glean what the reapers left behind alongside people she didn't know, in a brand new country she had never visited. This put her in a position to meet Boaz, who later married her and redeemed Naomi's husband's field, essentially reversing their fortunes for the better. But that only happened after Naomi coached Ruth on how to approach him.

The fact that so many writers, teachers, and preachers believe that "Wait for your Boaz" is the lesson here reflects our society's patriarchal tendencies more than it does biblical truth. The one thing Ruth definitely did *not* do was wait. She didn't stay in Moab to wait for a new husband. She didn't wait for a new life to find her or even for somebody to feed her. In the spirit of every resilient woman who's been served lemons, she thought creatively, used what she had, and made lemonade.

Here's where we find opportunities to learn from Ruth's story: How do we react when life slams us to the ground? When we lose loved ones, a job, or a relationship? We have to make a choice. Will we remain crushed under the weight of it all, or will we get up, rebuild, and choose to live? Becoming a widow at a young age was not the end of Ruth's story. She knew that with God's help there was life beyond that grief. Her life would never be the same, and perhaps neither will yours. But maybe you can move past the darkness of the moment, see what good things are waiting beyond the pain— and go after them.

Ultimately, Boaz did not change Ruth's life; she changed her own life. Her transformation happened in her mind long before she ever set foot on his field. Sure, he ended up marrying her and providing much-needed economic security for her and Naomi, but not until she went after her own stability. Boaz only contributed to a story Ruth had already started writing for herself. What new story will you write for yourself? Start with the one thing you know you can do, and *do that*.

Please turn to the next page for a JOURNAL PROMPT. ⋙➤

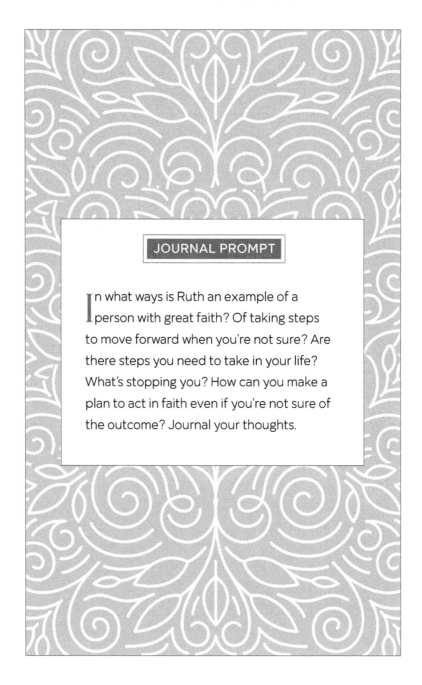

JOURNAL PROMPT

In what ways is Ruth an example of a person with great faith? Of taking steps to move forward when you're not sure? Are there steps you need to take in your life? What's stopping you? How can you make a plan to act in faith even if you're not sure of the outcome? Journal your thoughts.

NAOMI: GLORY AND GRIEF

She said to them, "Call me no longer Naomi, call me Mara, for the Almighty has dealt bitterly with me. I went away full, but the Lord has brought me back empty; why call me Naomi when the Lord has dealt harshly with me, and the Almighty has brought calamity upon me?"

RUTH 1:20–21

Nothing about Naomi's story is fair or easy. She lives through a famine, loses her husband and both her sons, has no grandchildren, uproots her life twice, and ends up back where she began. When we encounter her in this week's verses, newly returned to her hometown of Bethlehem, her grief is possibly at its most intense point. Forced to face her former community for the first time in years, she pours out her pain and embarrassment. *When I left, I had it all,* she says. *Now I'm returning because I lost everything.* Moreover, she identifies God as the culprit, the one who has been harsh to her and is responsible for all her tragedies. The heaviness is so much that she even demands a name change, from Naomi (which means "pleasant") to Mara (which means "bitter"), as if to say, *I'm not the woman you once knew. My sorrow has overcome me, and this is who I am now.*

Have you known any Maras? People who just can't seem to catch a break? No matter what they do, it seems they're constantly encountering loss, grief, and disappointment. It can be hard to watch and uncomfortable to listen to them. You may want to offer comfort, but the words don't come. They're hurting, and they're not going to be talked out of it— nor should they! This is where Naomi gives her first lesson in grief: Be honest about it, and allow those who are grieving to share how they really feel. Healing is in our truth-telling; there's something transformative about sharing our stories, because it means someone is listening to them.

But what is most powerful in this story is the fact that Naomi's friends listen to her without interrupting. They support her with their presence, but they don't try to fix her. Even if they wanted to, they couldn't, because ultimately, God is our fixer. God encounters us in the most painful of places to comfort, heal, and relieve. No human can provide that in the same way. When we sit in silence as those who grieve share their experiences, we leave room for God to enter, because we're not filling it up with our noise.

Naomi also learns the value of allowing people to be helpful in the ways they can. It's so easy to isolate ourselves when the pain of grief wrecks our souls. Naomi does this when she orders her daughters-in-law to return home, but

Ruth is determined to stay with Naomi to support her. After colliding with Ruth's fierce determination, Naomi concedes. And it ultimately works out for her, because later Ruth is able to work and secure some food and provisions for them.

As a mother figure, maybe Naomi felt *she* should be the one worried about someone else's life, needs, and future, not the other way around. But she had to learn that being cared for by a loving family was something *she* needed. You don't do yourself any favors by pushing away help. Being strong is not required all the time, nor should it be celebrated in all circumstances. Embracing your perceived weakness is what connects you to the love of community and the power of God. For God's grace is sufficient for you, and God's strength is made perfect in weakness (2 Corinthians 12:7–10).

WEEK 5

NAOMI'S JOY

[Ruth] bore a son. Then the women
said to Naomi, "Blessed be the Lord,
who has not left you this day without
next-of-kin; and may his name be
renowned in Israel! He shall be to you a
restorer of life and a nourisher of your
old age; for your daughter-in-law who
loves you, who is more to you than
seven sons, has borne him."
∾ RUTH 4:13–15

Last week, we talked about Naomi's circumstances at the
beginning of the book of Ruth and what God can teach us
about grief through her story. But by the end of the book,
Naomi is living a healed, happy life. She has moved through
her hour of grief and is embracing new life and all it can offer
her. In this week's verse, her community of girlfriends, who'd
stood with her in her darkest moments, now celebrate the
way God has turned her deepest sorrow into overwhelming

joy. She's gone from having lost her husband and children to becoming a grandmother to a child whose very existence nourishes her life. How did she get here? Rightly understood, the book of Ruth is actually just as much about Naomi, and it models the way we can overcome, persevere, and be resilient in very specific ways.

The first thing we notice in Naomi's journey is that grief itself is a form of prayer called "lament"—crying out to God in the midst of pain—and must be understood that way. In the scriptures, lament is one of the most powerful tools that Christians inherit from Jewish tradition. The book of Psalms is full of laments, and of course there's the book of Lamentations. This is no meaningless complaining. Rather, it demands the attention of the heavens and calls the Almighty to be witness to the turmoil of the lamenter. Lament flings itself toward heaven and refuses to be ignored.

So in her lamenting, Naomi teaches us that it's okay to cry out to God and require God's attention, modeling lament as an act of deep faith. These prayers are often full of the things we are most scared to say, which are also the things we need to say. And lament is productive; it allows us to cleanse ourselves of toxicity so we can move forward. The lesson here is to add lament as one of your spiritual tools that you intentionally access when you need it.

Look at what happens on the other side of this soul-cleansing prayer: Naomi is able to begin taking action, partnering with Ruth in ways that save both their lives. Back in Bethlehem, she is inspired by Ruth's gleaning efforts in the field, and she devises a plan to connect Ruth and Boaz, which ultimately secures both their futures. Had she still been holding all that bitterness from before, she wouldn't have been able to see what possibilities were in front of her. Bitterness and grief can be all-consuming, but setting them free to live in the open gives us some space to tend to other needs in our lives.

Before we know it, we've slowly but surely started reaching toward the hope of new life beyond grief. Note that the story doesn't end with Ruth and Boaz getting married. It goes on until the birth of their child, who becomes the joy of Naomi's life. And her friends help her see that God has not forgotten her. Even in her lowest moments, there was always hope. This child is evidence of that. Though Ruth bears him, the story is redeemed for Naomi when the baby is identified as Naomi's blessing. All the loss still hurts, but this child is hers to nurse, love, and nurture.

The lesson here: Get these kinds of friends! Friends who will listen to you and stand with you in times of lament but also celebrate with you in moments of triumph. And it's vital that we take time with our loved ones to acknowledge what God has done for us. Notice that the story isn't over until the narrative brings Naomi some redemption, pointing to God as the one who has blessed her and reversed her fortunes. If we lament and cry out during the painful times, we should also make time to celebrate, worship, and give thanks during the high times.

WEEK 6

A VERY PRESENT HELP

God is our refuge and strength, a very
present help in trouble. Therefore we
will not fear, though the earth should
change, though the mountains shake
in the heart of the sea; though its
waters roar and foam, though the
mountains tremble with its tumult.
∽ PSALM 46:1–3

We often begin at the wrong place when we find ourselves
in the midst of serious trouble. We often think about how
bad things are, how dark the moment, how painful the trial.
This leaves us stressed, worried, and overwhelmed. But the
psalmist who wrote these verses does something incredibly
important; they (I'm intentionally using gender-neutral pro-
nouns) reverse the order. Instead of starting with the trial
and offering the trial to God, they begin with God and offer
God to the trial.

What if our first thought in every moment and in every challenge was God? What if God was our starting place? Look closely at the text: Since God is present, helpful, strong, and a refuge for us, it doesn't really matter what comes our way. We won't fear it. Our awareness of what God can and will do shapes our perspective on everything. Sure, the earth will change form, the mountains will shake, and the water will roar and foam, but we aren't scared of any of that, because before any of that happened, we already knew God. And God was already present, helpful, strong, and a protector.

What if, rather than constantly telling God how the mountains are shaking and the world around you is crumbling, you also reminded yourself that God is present, helpful, strong, and your protection? To be sure, you *should* tell God about what you're going through, how you feel, and why you're scared. However, we are reminded in scripture to encourage ourselves in the Lord. What if your prayers shifted from simply telling God what's wrong to, like so many of the psalmists, reminding yourself of who God is and what God has promised you? Of course the mountains are shaking, but God is present and helpful. Of course my world is crumbling, but, God, you have promised to be with me.

I believe that God loves for us to pray the scriptures, quoting divine promises in our prayers. This encourages us and deepens faith. It turns the prayer of worry and fear into a statement of faith. It's a way of believing when we find it hard to do so. How would that deepen your faith? Strengthen your resolve? Encourage all those around you who look to you for leadership?

SCRIPTURE STUDY

- Make a list of all the verses you find encouraging during difficult times. (Feel free to search online!)

- Ask friends or loved ones to share their favorite scripture passages that help them during fearful or challenging times.

- Keep this list somewhere accessible.

- Consult this list and read some of these scriptures when you find yourself in a challenging time.

- During your prayer time, mention those promises of God found on your list. Let them encourage you and lead you to give thanks in prayer.

BENT BUT NOT BROKEN

And just then there appeared a
woman with a spirit that had crippled
her for eighteen years. She was bent
over and was quite unable to stand up
straight. When Jesus saw her, he called
her over and said, "Woman, you are set
free from your ailment."
∽ LUKE 13:11–12

Can you imagine the experience of this woman, bent over,
unable to stand up for 18 years? If she's a wife and mother, she
can't kiss her spouse or look into her children's eyes. Instead,
she looks at the ground all day. She no longer experiences the
simple joy of waking up in the morning and having a good
yawn and stretch. In fact, she hasn't been able to do much of
anything on her own. Someone has had to help her get in and
out of bed, bathe herself, get dressed. Her condition makes it
easy for people to overlook her, forget her, and exclude her
from normal social interactions.

But look at what happens. She shows up in the synagogue one day after having been ill for years, and Jesus sees her and heals her. Instantly, her life is changed. While her story speaks of an evil spirit that plagued her physically, it might be helpful for us to consider what plagues us spiritually or emotionally. What are the things that weigh us down psychologically and keep us from enjoying the beautiful, abundant life we so desire? What heartache, anger, or bitterness is standing in the way of our joy, peace, and faith? And what does this woman's story tell us we can do about it?

The most important step this woman takes in changing her own narrative is to get herself to the place and to the person who could help her: Jesus. It had to be uncomfortable and inconvenient, but she made her way to the synagogue. Perhaps she had heard people talking about Jesus and how he was healing people of their physical ailments. She did not hide behind the stigma placed on her but rather brought herself right into his presence. He saw her and he healed her. In the text she doesn't say one word, but her actions demonstrate to her entire community, to herself, and to Jesus that she's ready for a change.

The same is true for us. If we want healing from all the social, emotional, and spiritual weights that burden us and leave us bent over, we can bring them to God in prayer, in devotion time, or wherever we meet the Almighty. Doing so is an invitation to God to come and meet us at the point of our need. Showing up before God, not being ashamed of where we are but just bringing the raw honesty of our predicament, opens us to divine power and love. Welcoming our vulnerability, God responds to the sincere offering, embracing us fully and working to set us free.

WEEK 8

BEAUTY FOR ASHES

To console those who mourn in Zion,
To give them beauty for ashes,
The oil of joy for mourning,
The garment of praise for the spirit
of heaviness.
∽ ISAIAH 61:3 (NKJV)

It had been about six months since we'd broken up, but you wouldn't have known it. We were still doing all the things that couples do: going on dates, talking on the phone, texting. But I was far from happy in love. The cycle of pain I willingly participated in with him left me wounded over and over again. I could almost pinpoint when the tide would turn. We'd be together, enjoy each other's company, go on a few dates. Then he would go silent, and I would be left hurt. A few days later, like the morning sun, he would come back. I was safe and sure, a place he could always return to once he was ready. Longing to keep the connection and unable to face the reality of the loss, I would allow him back. It was draining. It was painful. But it was mine.

It wasn't like I didn't know I was making a mistake. I knew this was going to keep hurting me, but I kept choosing it anyway. I knew I needed to walk away, but I had no idea how. Before we "broke up," we had been so in love. I told my girlfriend, my voice cracking through the tears, "I've waited forever to feel like this about somebody, and now I have to give it up?" And for six more months, I didn't. I couldn't.

Have you ever been there? Stuck in a place so unhealthy, so draining, that it almost becomes dangerous. Carrying around the corpse of a long-dead relationship shifts your mental and emotional state. It's over and you know it, but you can't fully admit that to yourself or bring yourself to bury it.

During those months, I was desperately sad all the time. I would get just enough energy to go to work and go home to sleep. Occasionally, if I had to preach, God's anointing would fall and give me what I needed to get through the assignment, but afterward, I'd be right back in the throes of depression. Those were really dark days, but in time, God snatched me back from the despair that had overcome me.

I started attending a small group at church that was focused on breaking bad habits. One of my group members pointed out the fact that not only was I fiercely protecting and carrying around the ashes of my dead relationship, but whenever I managed to drop them, I'd just sweep them back up and hold on to them again. That was so true! That's when God made a deal with me: If I gave God my ashes, God would give me beauty in exchange, just like in this week's Bible verse. Though I didn't know how to let go, I told God that the next time I dropped the ashes of my relationship—the next time my sort-of-ex-boyfriend disappeared—I would not pick them up. I would finally accept that it was really over.

And, like clockwork, it happened. He went silent again, on Valentine's Day of all times. It hurt, but I knew that was my moment. That was my chance to, for once, let the ashes lie there and walk away. By the grace of God, I did just that, and the beauty God has given me in the years since has been more incredible than I can express. These days, I have lasting love, joy in my work, and the deepest contentment I've known. Everything isn't perfect, but it is genuine.

What ashes do you need to let fall to the ground for good? What beauty are you missing out on because you're still grasping the dead things that can do you no good? Consider giving the ashes back to God. Trust the Lord to lift the heaviness and make way for more joy, more beauty, more peace, more love, more of everything you need.

WEEK 9

COURAGE IN ACTION: FROM PRIVILEGED TO EMPOWERED

Mordecai told them to reply to Esther,
"Do not think that in the king's palace
you will escape any more than all the
other Jews.... Who knows? Perhaps
you have come to royal dignity for just
such a time as this."
∽ ESTHER 4:13–14

The book of Esther has all the makings of a great story:
protagonist, antagonist, humor, conflict, rich characters,
compelling storylines, truth, and valuable life lessons. Esther
starts as a Jewish orphan girl living far from her homeland
in the Persian empire. She doesn't have much power, but she
has a loving mentor and surrogate parent in her older cousin,
Mordecai, and she finds favor with Hegai, an officer of the
king's court, during a yearlong royal beauty contest. Both help

Esther navigate her road to royalty, and without even trying very hard, Esther gains the affections of King Ahasuerus (also known as Xerxes) and takes her place as queen of Persia.

However, as in any good story, no sooner does she step into her new role than trouble heads her way. One of the king's top officials, Haman, is angry that Mordecai—who, as a faithful Jew, will only bow before God—refuses to bow before him. To take revenge, he craftily manipulates the king into issuing a decree that all Jews in the kingdom be put to death.

As the date when the genocidal policy will take effect draws near, Esther is faced with a decision. No one knows that the queen is Jewish (including the king) and that this policy will affect her people, so she needs to speak up. But death is a possible penalty for anyone who approaches the king without invitation, including the queen. Will she intervene? *Can* she intervene? What will it cost her if she does, and is she willing to pay the price? Whose safety and comfort will she prioritize—her own or her people's?

If you dare to reach for destiny, you, too, will face this kind of defining moment. If you're going to take a leadership position, at some point you must show what kind of leader you'll be. It's not enough to claim the role. Who will you be *in* the role? Will you choose integrity over insecurity? Courage over comfort? That kind of choice is where character is formed and faith is deepened.

Thankfully, Esther chooses well, modeling for us how to do the same. Moving in courage, Esther leverages her privilege as queen and speaks up. When King Ahasuerus learns the truth behind Haman's murderous plot, he puts a stop to it. Because Esther was willing to enter the room and to make a difference once she got there, she saved countless lives and turned the Jewish people's fate around for the better.

Esther's example encourages us not to celebrate the sacrifice of the individual for the community but rather to see ourselves as *part of* our communities, deeply connected to their fate. What privilege do you have? At what tables do you sit? What rooms do you enter that grant you access to decision- and policy-making that can give relief to those who suffer? Speaking up may cost you something, personally or professionally, but it may also deliver justice for your community, give new purpose to your work, and maybe even change the world. Don't underestimate your ability to effect change. Perhaps you aren't the queen of Persia, but who knows? Maybe God placed you where you are for a purpose, for such a time as this, just like Esther.

Please turn to the next page for a JOURNAL PROMPT. ≫→

JOURNAL PROMPT

Journal your thoughts on the following questions.

Have there been times when you felt you should have spoken up on behalf of others but chose not to? What stopped you? How can you follow Esther's example the next time you have a chance? Think about a time you *did* speak up on behalf of others. What did it feel like? What difference did it make? Would you do it again?

What does Esther teach you about privilege? Can you make a list of some privileges you live with? How can you take advantage of them in order to help someone else?

WEEK 10

ESTHER ENTHRONED: LIFE ON THE OTHER SIDE OF COURAGE

On that day King Ahasuerus gave to
Queen Esther the house of Haman,
the enemy of the Jews; and Mordecai
came before the king, for Esther had
told what he was to her.
∾ ESTHER 8:1

In last week's devotion, we discussed how Esther risked her
own life to use the privilege she had to save her people from
Haman's genocidal plot. What happens next? Haman is put
to death, and everything he owned is given to Esther. But she
still has work to do. Haman's murderous decree is still in place
and legally can't be reversed, meaning that, at a date in the
near future, all the Jews in the Persian empire are still sched-
uled to be put to death. So Esther returns to the king, this time
boldly and confidently. Armed with the king's endorsement,

she opens the way for Mordecai to write a royal decree giving the Jews the legal right to fight back against their attackers. When the day comes, the Jews are triumphant and easily win the day. Not satisfied with this victory, Esther crafts a new decree, allowing the Jews in the capital city of Susa to fight one more day, which the king is happy to sign.

Look at what God did for Esther when she activated her courage! Esther went from being a quiet, obedient queen, unsure of her own power and place, to being a cultural leader who was innovative, strategic, and politically savvy. Not only did she successfully try her hand at crafting public policy, she also managed property, appointed and supervised leaders, advised the king, established an annual celebration (the Jewish holiday Purim), and ultimately became a political force in the empire and a prominent figure of her people. At once, she represented the state and a powerful minority *within* the state. In this way, Esther became a valuable and trusted partner to the king, demonstrating her leadership capacity, intelligence, and bravery.

Esther's narrative teaches us that acting in courage will reveal who we are, shining a light on our character and the value we can bring to a space. When you do the courageous thing, you might shock yourself and uncover new talents, strengths, and abilities you didn't know you had. Esther was once terrified to even approach the king, her own husband, but by the end of the story, he was signing policies she had written. The experience of risking her life for what was right transformed her and got her past the fear that would have ultimately rendered her useless as queen—just another name and title, devoid of influence. Instead, she went from worrying about all the things she shouldn't do to thinking of all the things she *could* do—and doing them.

That's the place within yourself where confidence, compassion, smarts, and service can combine, and you find yourself doing some of your best work. It's knowing in the pit of your stomach what you're capable of and not being afraid to go for it. That kind of powerful, focused, courageous action will always be attention-getting, especially to other leaders and decision-makers. And God will ultimately put you in the spaces that are big enough for your talents and presence, even if you have to occasionally journey through spaces that aren't. Where can courage take you? Are you willing to go? Will you trust God and yourself on the journey? The greatness that is in us doesn't come out because we desire it so. It comes out because we require it so.

WEEK 11

VASHTI: A PREQUEL

After these things, when the anger
of King Ahasuerus had abated, he
remembered Vashti and what she had
done and what had been decreed
against her.
∽ ESTHER 2:1

It should have been his highest moment as king, but instead,
the shadow of disappointment and the sobering reality of
divorce hung over his head.

For six months, King Ahasuerus had been celebrating his
wealth and power with lavish banquets for all the nobles in
the Persian empire. His wife, Queen Vashti, hosted her own
amazing soirée for the women of Susa, the capital, inside the
royal palace. As grand as this was, the king wanted more.
Deep into his merriment (and after much drinking), he
invited his queen to come before him and all his drunk friends
to show off her beauty—likely naked, wearing only her crown,

according to Katharine Doob Sakenfeld in *Just Wives?: Stories of Power and Survival in the Old Testament and Today.*

Vashti refused. King Ahasuerus was livid. Embarrassed publicly by his defiant wife, he felt the social pressure to *do* something. Advised by his top counselors, he not only dismissed her as queen but also sent messengers throughout the empire to declare that this kind of wifely disobedience would not be tolerated by any man, certainly not the king. But later, in his quiet moments, the king thought about Queen Vashti. When we read this week's verse, we can't be sure what he was thinking or feeling. Did he have regrets? Did he love and miss her?

If we allowed Queen Vashti to speak for herself, what would she say? We don't have much to go on. We don't even know the exact reason she refused to come when the king called her. For the lessons God wants us to learn through Queen Vashti, perhaps it's best that we are never told, because we are given a chance to imagine them for ourselves.

The first lesson is that "No" is a complete sentence. It requires no accompanying explanation or validation. The truth is, it didn't matter why the queen refused to come. What mattered was she wasn't coming. She gave herself the power to make a choice for herself, and she was at peace with the choice she made. She wasn't concerned with who wouldn't like it or what the fallout would be. Her no meant no.

By acting with this kind of boldness and conviction, Queen Vashti single-handedly upset the balance of power in the empire, forcing the men to step back and think about what kind of society this would be and who they would be as men. They actually had a crisis meeting to discuss the matter at length (Esther 1:13–21). Even though they chose patriarchy over equality, it is significant that through her simple act of resistance, Vashti unwittingly forced their hand and demanded that they choose. She had dared to defy the king and, in so doing, changed the world. Her resistance was met with severe punishment, but it also set an important precedent. She had proven that a queen could defy the king and live, opening the door for Esther to later go to King Ahasuerus without being called and fulfill God's plan to save her people.

And this is the most important lesson we can learn from Vashti: Sometimes it may cost you a lot to stand up for what you believe. However, there is grace in that. If, for Vashti, appearing naked in front of her husband and his officials was inconsistent with her values, then being dismissed for refusing to do so was the best thing that could have happened to her. Having to live in an environment where your convictions, voice, and personhood are not respected is not to live at all.

Moreover, we won't always be given credit for righteous action. In fact, no one in the story, not even the narrator, celebrates Vashti's bold action, which God used to put a divine plan in motion. That task is left for us to do today in our telling of and reflecting on the story. If no one ever calls our names for the good we've done, we should choose what we know to be right and feel good about that, regardless of the consequences. When you act on your personal convictions, know that you're setting a powerful example for those who run alongside you and those who come after you.

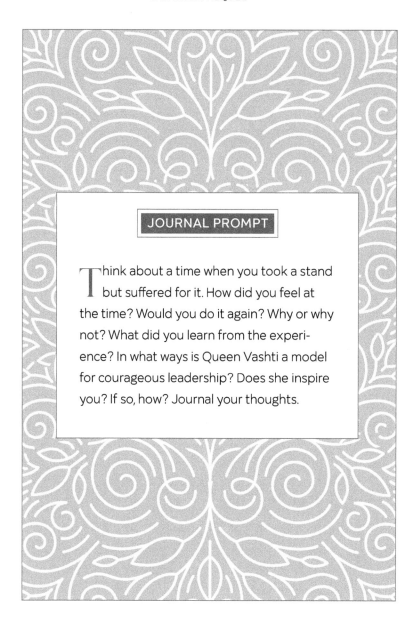

JOURNAL PROMPT

Think about a time when you took a stand but suffered for it. How did you feel at the time? Would you do it again? Why or why not? What did you learn from the experience? In what ways is Queen Vashti a model for courageous leadership? Does she inspire you? If so, how? Journal your thoughts.

WEEK 12

THE SHULAMITE'S GREAT ADVICE

I adjure you, O daughters of Jerusalem,
do not stir up or awaken love until it
is ready!
∾ SONG OF SOLOMON 8:4

The Song of Solomon is the only love poem in the Bible. Dripping with erotic imagery, it celebrates love, sexual intimacy, and the passions that lie therein. It's also the only book of the Bible in which a woman's voice is dominant. Still, the collection of poems shares passionate dialogue between two people, a woman known as the Shulamite and her lover, who describe with joy their desire for each other, their sexual sharing, and their hopes for love. Though we don't know much about her, other than that she's probably from a place called Shulem, the Shulamite takes us on an intimate journey as she reflects with her lover on their experience of walking through the flames of love. It's thrilling to read and leaves her audience—both the reader and the "daughters of Jerusalem" in the poem—inspired to experience our own passionate journeys.

So why does she tell us on three different occasions (Song of Solomon 2:7, 3:5, 8:4) *not* to awaken love before it is ready? She goes on about how in love she is, how intoxicating love is, and how pleasing the feeling is, but then, every so often, she says, *But don't fall in love until the time is right!* Why?

Though our heroine never answers those questions plainly, she offers several poetic clues. First of all, love is all-consuming. She says multiple times that she is faint with love, utterly lovesick. Love has a way of taking over, disrupting your life and demanding all your attention. The object of our affection can become everything to us, and this can be dangerous. We can't sit and stare into the eyes of our beloved all day, every day. It can easily become worship rather than affection, even idolatrous. Our relationships should not become all of life but should inspire us to live better. In this way, being in love has to be navigated with care and maturity.

Moreover, not all seasons of life allow us to welcome this kind of disorienting excitement without damaging other important aspects of life: faith, family, our purpose. Our world loves to tell us we can have it all, but, as Renita J. Weems points out in her book *What Matters Most: Ten Lessons in Living Passionately from the Song of Solomon,* maybe we can't—at least not all at the same time. By suggesting that there's a "right time" for love, the Shulamite implies that there's a *wrong* time for love. We can only be prayerful about when that time is and seek to discern God's direction. Maybe we discern it correctly; maybe we don't. But it's definitely valuable to ask God if we're ready and if our beloved is ready. Because sometimes we're not; they're not. And that's a recipe for heartbreak. Feeling love is one thing, but tending a relationship is another. Falling in love before we're ready to show up for a relationship will inevitably hurt us or someone else.

And because love is "strong as death" (Song of Solomon 8:6), it can be nearly impossible to walk away when we should. So if you know you can't be emotionally available or mature enough to handle all that comes with love (vulnerability, open communication, working through problems, extending love and care, and generally being of service to another person), it's best to wait until you are. The Shulamite speaks from experience, and her advice is worthy of real consideration.

What is most important to note in the Shulamite's counsel is that, ultimately, love is a choice. While we often speak of "falling" in love because of how it feels, we do make the decision to do it. And if we're choosing to love, we need to own that choice rather than pretending it just happened to us. What questions will you ask yourself to be sure you're ready for love? Will you choose it this time? Or will you wait until the time is right?

WEEK 13

DESTINED FOR MORE

A mustard seed . . . is the smallest of all
the seeds on earth; yet when it is sown
it grows up and becomes the greatest
of all shrubs, and puts forth large
branches, so that the birds of the air
can make nests in its shade.
∾ MARK 4:31–32

This passage is an insightful teaching of Jesus. He shows how
the smallest seed, when planted, grows into a massive shrub
whose branches provide sanctuary for the birds. Jesus shows
that this is what it's like to have faith in God, to be part of the
Kingdom of God and to experience the transformative work
God is doing in those who believe. Much like the mustard
seed, there is much we can glean from this brief parable.

First, we note that size does not matter. The mustard seed
is small indeed, but that doesn't mean it's not destined for
greatness. Who would think that a seed the size of a fleck
of ground pepper could transform into something as large

and purposeful as the mustard shrub? But it does. Have you ever sabotaged your future by downplaying your talents, abilities, and sense of purpose and destiny? There are enough naysayers who don't believe in where you're going and who you're growing into. Don't you dare add to their chorus, helping them sing their song of unbelief.

Second, we know that it takes time for this transformation to happen; a shrub doesn't grow overnight. But if we're patient and submit to the growth process that God has invited in us, we will emerge wiser, better, and far more resourceful than we ever thought we could be. Have you ever uprooted yourself from the places where you had been planted, preventing yourself from developing? We have to get settled somewhere in soil that can nourish us so that we can progress. Sometimes you just have to decide to "bloom where you're planted." Rather than getting frustrated because you're not seeing the results you'd like, what if you were determined to trust God and pray through the process, believing that your transformation was on the way? How would that change your life? How would it shape your experiences?

Remember that, once planted, the mustard seed has no choice but to become the shrub. That's what it was always meant to be. It was destined for more from the beginning. The same is true for you. You are more than what people see. They cannot even fathom the greatness, the majesty that is within you. So get yourself planted where God leads you within the body of Christ, and let God transform your seed into a big, beautiful, bountiful shrub.

PART II

LIVING WATER FROM THE WELL: INTIMACY WITH GOD

Jesus answered her, "If you knew the
gift of God, and who it is that is saying
to you, 'Give me a drink,' you would
have asked him, and he would have
given you living water."
∽ JOHN 4:10

The story of the Samaritan woman at the well, found in John 4, is a controversial text. There has been much debate about the encounter between this unnamed woman and Jesus, the content of their exchange, what is really happening here, and why. What starts as a simple request for water turns into a deep theological discussion that motivates the woman to testify about what she experienced to anyone who will listen.

Who is this woman? As a Samaritan, she was part of a minority group, an outcast from the Jewish religious establishment, yet she had a sense of cultural pride—she couldn't wait to mention that the well she was drawing from had been given to the Samaritans by their ancestor Jacob. Still, she desired more from God and was open to engaging across cultural and religious differences to find it.

While you might be happy to go about your normal daily activities, I bet that, like the Samaritan woman, you also want more in life. You want a life that means something, a faith that accomplishes something. Thankfully, what lies at the core of this exchange is a framework for experiencing intimacy with God—the kind of intimacy that readies us for the higher meaning we're so thirsty for.

The Samaritan woman shows us that Jesus desires the same intimacy with us that we do with him. It was no accident that he came to the well in Samaria. Though they were a religious minority, Jesus reached out to them—and he reaches out to us in much the same way. He stops in our neighborhoods and engages us, tempting us with living water that promises to satisfy our deepest thirst forever. Will we take a drink?

Her story also shows that intimacy with God means willingness to have our routines interrupted. If we feel the Lord nudging us, we need to take a minute to listen. It won't always be in our planned devotional time that God speaks to us. It might be while we're at work or trying to sleep or going about our daily chores, like the Samaritan woman was. It may be at what seems to be the most inconvenient time. Welcome the interruption. The living water Jesus gives will satisfy our parched souls.

Finally, the kind of intimacy the woman at the well experienced is rooted in honesty and vulnerability. Many people assume that when Jesus mentions her list of former lovers, he's trying to shame her, but that's not what it says in the text. So why does Jesus bring it up? First, it allows him to speak a truth to her about her life, signifying the ways that we can all be honest with God because God knows our truth anyway. Furthermore, Jesus uses this moment as a way for the woman to know him. Look at her response. As soon as he recounts her life's history, she says, "Sir, I perceive that you are a prophet!" Suddenly, she understands that Jesus is not just some thirsty stranger. She moves from being annoyed with his carrying on about living water to understanding that he looks into her life and knows her intimately. Jesus wants to do the same with us: to be known and loved by us, all while satisfying us with water that nourishes us forever. How do we open ourselves to this kind of intimacy? How do we say yes to this living water?

WEEK 15

GOD SEES ME!

So she named the Lord who spoke to
her, "You are El-roi"; for she said, "Have
I really seen God and remained alive
after seeing him?"
∾ GENESIS 16:13

Hagar's experience with God is one of the most captivating
in scripture. While her story is often told with Abraham and
Sarah at the center, womanist theologian Delores S. Williams
writes beautifully about Hagar's perspective in her work *Sisters in the Wilderness: The Challenge of Womanist God-Talk*.
Though Hagar only appears in a couple of chapters in the
Bible, her story shows us how God intervenes in our situations to extend love and grace.

Although God has promised that Abraham will become the
father of many nations, Sarah and Abraham are old and have
yet to conceive any children. Old Testament scholar Gerhard
von Rad writes in his commentary on Genesis, "There was no
greater sorrow for an Israelite . . . woman than childlessness."

It was so important, in fact, that there was a cultural practice that allowed a woman in Sarah's position to have her husband father a child with her maid. The maid's children would be considered the original wife's, not the maid's. We should be clear that "maid" here really means "slave-girl." The maid had no choice in the matter. And unfortunately, this is the arrangement that Sarah makes for Abraham and Hagar so that she can have children. What a painful situation Hagar is in: She has no control over her life or her body. She has to marry Abraham and conceive his child and has no room to object.

Hagar gets pregnant by Abraham but fails to properly humble herself before her owner Sarah (Genesis 16:4). This sets Sarah off. Thus, she "dealt harshly" with Hagar. *Anah*, the Hebrew word translated here as "dealt harshly," is the same word used in the Bible to describe the experience of the Israelites at the hands of the Egyptians, so we know it's pretty bad—so bad that Hagar runs away from Sarah into the wilderness. She has no money, no food, no help of any kind. The likelihood that she and the baby growing inside her will survive is getting dangerously low. What will she do?

Perhaps you can relate to Hagar. Maybe you have no peace at home, or your family is at odds and you can't seem to heal from past hurts. Perhaps you feel abandoned by loved ones, or maybe you suffered violence at the hands of someone who was supposed to love you. Maybe you ran away from this desolate situation only to find that you, like Hagar, had no support or resources.

But when Hagar's death seems almost certain, the Lord shows up and initiates a conversation with her. God listens to her story and sends her back to Abraham and Sarah—which might seem like an unfavorable option for Hagar, until you realize that God is ensuring that she and her child survive. God is also securing her future, promising to give her a son and to multiply her offspring. And if we look closer at what happens, we can find incredible power and encouragement for our own lives.

The most encouraging part of this story is the way this experience with God proves to be absolutely life-changing for Hagar. Old Testament scholar Phyllis Trible notes that Hagar is the only person in the Bible who has the distinction of naming God. In verse 13, she says, "Have I really seen God and remained alive?" and names God *El-Roi,* which in Hebrew means "the God who sees." What this means is that Hagar's ultimate realization in all that she experienced was *God sees me!*

God saw the danger she and her child were in and acted to protect them. When she had run out of options and had no place to go, God took notice and acted on her behalf. The same is true for us. God has not missed a single event in our lives. God sees us and responds with compassion to help us.

GUIDED REFLECTION

How important is it to feel seen—by God, by loved ones, by people in general? What is the result if we don't? Who are the people who make you feel seen? How did/do they do so? How can you follow their example and help others feel seen?

WEEK 16

FEAR ME, I AM FABULOUS

For it was you who formed my inward
parts; you knit me together in my
mother's womb. I praise you, for I
am fearfully and wonderfully made.
Wonderful are your works; that I know
very well.
∽ PSALM 139:13–14

There is something in this verse, which claims that we are fearfully and wonderfully made, that is simply exciting to read. In fact, it's more than a verse you read; it's one you *feel*. Impressively, in this psalm, the psalmist exudes and embodies confidence, sass, and humility simultaneously. If you sit with it for long, it can have you feeling especially good about yourself. But why? And what could it possibly mean to be *fearfully* made? Beautifully made, sure. Perhaps even thoughtfully made. But fearfully? What does that mean? She (I'm choosing to read the psalmist as a woman as a way to help women see ourselves in the text) has much to teach us here if we but listen.

Much like other scriptures that describe the beautiful work of God—sun, moon, stars, flowers, sky, oceans, and trees—in this verse, our psalmist walks herself to center stage to tell of her own greatness. Just as visible and as much a part of creation as anything else, she finds it necessary to celebrate the fact that she, too, was designed and formed by an incredible God. She is the work of the greatest artist of all time, and just the knowledge of that causes praise to pour out of her heart.

We must be careful not to read this as arrogance. Quite the opposite—it's coming to terms with the source of one's very being and being amazed by it. *I was made by the most amazing Creator who made everything. God, I praise you for crafting, shaping, and obviously desiring me.* What would happen if we let that truth seep into the core of our being? That we are beautiful because we were made by the Most Beautiful One? And that One desired us to be and so created us, and here we are. What does that do for your self-esteem? For your sense of purpose? How does it root you in love? You were wanted, and so God made you.

The second thing our psalmist teaches us is to expect others to celebrate that God has made us (and what that means) just as much as we do. The word translated as "fearfully" is the Hebrew word *nora*, meaning "inspiring reverence, godly fear, or awe." In other words, she's saying, *Be in awe of me—not for me, but out of respect to the One who made me.* You have been crafted by God in a way that requires reverence for what God has done in artfully making you. This reverence is yours to give *and* yours to receive from those around you. To take anything less is to undermine the reverence you bring yourself. You are a piece of God's most prized art; cherish that truth and require it of others. Let this shape the way you choose relationships and the way you spend your time.

JOB'S WIFE

Then his wife said to him, "Do you still persist in your integrity? Curse God, and die."
∽ JOB 2:9

Life is often ugly, painful, and unfair. And perhaps no story better captures this reality than Job's. He begins as a rich man, wealthy in material things, family, and friends. He's a faithful man who shares a life with his wife, whom he loves deeply (Job 19:17). They live a joyous life together until it all ends abruptly: They lose their wealth, everything they own, and their 10 children through a combination of theft, fire, and a tornado. And unbeknownst to them, all these tragic events come at the hand of Satan, because God wants to prove to Satan just how righteous his servant Job is. It would be a bitter pill to swallow for anyone, but it seems especially so for Job's wife. In the second round of tests, Job breaks out in boils all over his body, losing even his health. This is when Job's wife issues her stunningly hopeless and pessimistic advice:

Stop holding on to your integrity any further. Just curse God and die. That will put you out of your own misery.

Her words leap off the page as cold, mean, and unsupportive and have solidified her reputation as an antihero within the story and in Christian tradition. She's not presented as a faithful, pious woman, and she clearly doesn't subscribe to the ride-or-die mentality. But, in all fairness, she has lost nearly everything Job has lost. Women in these times were dependent on men for survival; without sons and with her husband too sick to work, she's destitute. Will they starve? Will they die? Things are bad for them both.

Also note that Job's wife watched everything play out as the closest person to him. What might it have done to her to watch this tragedy in real time? Maybe her words were expressing the dire state of her own spirit. Rather than offer her husband words of comfort or encouragement that she doesn't have, she can only manage to pour out the despair in her own heart: *Give up, Job. Why go on being righteous, serving a God who abandoned you—abandoned us—like this?*

In this moment of utter despair and raw transparency, Job's wife points to the critical choice we all have to make in life sometimes. How will we respond when life attacks us with its most vicious blows? What will be our answer? Do we cling to hope? Beg for mercy? Seethe in anger? Do we search for answers? Demand justice? Do we blame God? Ourselves? Others?

Most importantly, do we turn toward God, or do we walk away from God? Should we let life's circumstances sever our relationship with God? Is that justified or wise? Job says no. Though he's experiencing his deepest despair, he refuses to walk away from God and stop being the righteous person he always has been. He has questions and complaints, and he boldly takes them directly to God. Good for him, but perhaps his wife just can't get there. She is a grieving mother, likely too overcome with pain to even look for hope, let alone offer some to her spouse. We can't be entirely sure of the lasting power of her despair. Do her words represent a permanent end to her own spirituality? Or is this a temporary moment of lament? She never reappears in the story, so we can't know what ultimately happened with her, but we can decide what will happen with us.

Living will absolutely involve pain and sometimes indescribable loss. Our response should always be honest, as Job's wife's was, letting the pain pour out like a song, an offering to God. However, the caveat is this: Rather than allow that pain to destroy our fellowship with God, we should seek ways to allow the pain to strengthen it. There cannot be any good thing on the other side of walking away from God; that is spiritual death and can only make matters worse for us. Instead, run toward God and offer all the bitterness to the One who has promised to be our refuge and available help in difficult times.

Please turn to the next page for a GUIDED PRAYER. ≫→

GUIDED PRAYER

Lord, I do not understand this pain or the fact that you have allowed it. But I also know you promised to be with me always. Be strong in me. Guide me through this trial like you guided Job. Brighten the way and let me feel your love. I really don't understand this, and it feels so unfair! But I need you to bring me through it. Be my friend and companion in this difficult moment. Draw me closer to you. Open my heart to your love. Amen.

WEEK 18

AN ANTIDOTE FOR THE PAIN

Create in me a clean heart, O God, and put a new and right spirit within me. Do not cast me away from your presence, and do not take your holy spirit from me. Restore to me the joy of your salvation, and sustain in me a willing spirit.
∽ PSALM 51:10–12

Job's wife's pain, as described in last week's devotion, is deep, heavy, and very human. She lost everything, and her words are proof she wasn't handling it well. While she shows us the importance of being honest about our pain, she also shows us what can happen when we don't process or deal with it. We can lash out and take our hurt out on those we love most, those we'd never want to hurt. To be sure, she was overwhelmed and emotionally spent, so we can easily understand the low state of her heart and mind. But if she were to find a way out of that place, what would that look like? How could she turn toward God instead of away from God? How do you do that in a moment like this?

Enter Psalm 51. Though many believe it to be a psalm of David, written after his affair with Bathsheba and his indirect murder of her husband, it can be useful for more than just confession. This psalm invites God to transform the heart. It doesn't matter what its condition is or how it got there, God is capable of creating your heart anew. What if, in the midst of the heaviness we feel, we stopped to recognize just how bad things are inside us—and told God the truth about it, inviting God to the pain? *God, my heart is in a horrible place. It's ugly, and I can't fix it. I don't like how I feel, and I barely recognize myself. The only way things will get better is if you restore me from the inside out. Please help me by giving me a new heart and renewing my spirit. If I could do it myself, I would, but I can't. Only you can help.*

These are the kinds of prayers that transform lives, restore fortunes, and brighten futures. More importantly, they deepen our relationships with the divine—simple, direct, honest, vulnerable. We don't have to lie about what we feel, but we also don't have to stay there, and we don't have to allow our pain to poison us. It starts with an invitation, requesting God to come and fix it, to fix *us*. Realizing we can't do it alone can be hard, but if we do it, we become all the better for it, as it opens us to God's creative and healing power. However, the prayer doesn't end there; it also extends an invitation to God for companionship on the journey. If our anger and pain have caused us to walk away from God, the blessed part is that, as long as we have breath, we can mend that brokenness and

AN ANTIDOTE FOR THE PAIN

reconnect with our Creator. And this is where we find restoration of our joy and spiritual renewal.

This psalm is a beautiful one that affirms what we have always wanted to be true: Nothing can really separate us from God's love. Even when life's circumstances imprison us in despair, we can always reconnect, find hope, and start over again. If you find yourself in a dark, ugly place, as Job's wife did, let this prayer lead you to the beauty and the light of God's love. Say the words. God is always ready to respond. "Create in me a clean heart, O God, and put a new and right spirit within me."

OUR LEG OF THE RACE

I am reminded of your sincere
faith, a faith that lived first in your
grandmother Lois and your mother
Eunice and now, I am sure, lives in you.
For this reason I remind you to rekindle
the gift of God that is within you
through the laying on of my hands.
∞ 2 TIMOTHY 1:5–6

In this passage, Paul, who is likely writing this letter from prison, is reaching out to Timothy, his protégé, to encourage him in the faith and in his role as a leader in the church. Timothy was very special to Paul; in fact, he calls Timothy "beloved." When he thinks about the future of the church and how it will fare, he thinks of Timothy. As a passionate mentor and guide to Timothy, Paul is likely concerned for him and for his commitment to the gospel within the challenging times of his day. Some of those challenges were related to countering the spread of false doctrine and strife within and outside the church. Paul wants to be sure Timothy is able to stand strong in these times, in his own faith and as a faith leader. But why is this important to us? And why does Paul mention Timothy's mom and grandma?

There are a few things we can learn from this passage if we consider it closely. Paul knows firsthand the challenges of staying committed to the work of God, especially when it seems like the world around you is going crazy. If we're not careful, we can become so discouraged by what we see happening within the faith community (moral failings, lack of commitment, lack of spirituality, even discrimination—and silence about all that) as well as outside it (divisive politics, violence, racism, sexism) that we actually want to disengage. When it seems we're fighting an uphill battle alone, we can be disheartened despite our best efforts. But here is where Paul advises Timothy to do two things: (1) Remember where you've come from, and (2) use that to tap into who you really are and activate the gift of God inside you.

While it's true that Timothy is Paul's protégé, Paul is careful to acknowledge the true source of Timothy's faithful upbringing: his mother and grandmother, Eunice and Lois. They have laid a great foundation of faith for Timothy that grafts him onto an important legacy. Sometimes a look back at the stories of our ancestors (family or not) can reorient us to our strength and purpose. We remember that we are part of a larger story and that we must complete our leg of the race, just as those who've gone before us did. If they did it, we can, too. For it is their examples of triumph that provide inspiration and a blueprint to carry on the work to which we have each been called.

And what is the content of that blueprint exactly? What is the source of inspiration that moves us from apathy to action, from pessimism to purpose? The Holy Spirit, of course! Like Timothy, we can rekindle the gift of God inside us. We can allow the Holy Spirit to move and breathe within us, fanning the fire inside from a tiny flicker into a fruitful flame. What this shows is that God has already placed a gift inside us all, and it has not burned out. At any time, we can choose to rekindle it, to fan it into flame, to reconnect to our power and stand in our greatness. If we get discouraged sometimes, that's okay. But we shouldn't give up. Just recharge and come back as powerful and focused as ever.

GUIDED REFLECTION

Take a moment to reflect on the awesomeness of your elders and ancestors. Who were/are they? Who were the ones who taught you words of prayer, scripture, the meaning of faith and of life? Who offered prayers on your behalf? Reflect on those people and pause to give thanks. Say their names. Write them letters. Express your gratitude. It will do your soul good and inspire you for days to come.

MORE LIKE MARY

But the Lord answered her, "Martha, Martha, you are worried and distracted by many things; there is need of only one thing. Mary has chosen the better part, which will not be taken away from her."

⁓ LUKE 10:41–42

Tucked away in the book of Luke is this brief exchange among Mary, Martha, and Jesus. Jesus and all his friends have been traveling and decide to stop by Martha's house. She immediately springs into hostess mode, doing a lot of work to properly host these special visitors. Her sister Mary opts to sit at Jesus's feet and listen to him talk. This makes Martha very upset, and she voices her complaint to Jesus. She feels her sister should be helping her prepare for hosting.

Mary says nothing in the text itself, but if she were to tell her story, she might say something like this:

I love my sister. I really do. But I often feel as if she just doesn't get me. I never intended to abandon her to do all the housework that day, though I admit I wasn't particularly helpful. She's right. I sat there at Jesus's feet and listened to him. He had so much wisdom to pour out, so much insight to share. He was encouraging, insightful, loving, funny, smart, and honest. I couldn't help but listen. I knew she was getting frustrated. I could hear her sighing loudly and slamming pots, but I just couldn't move. I was captured by the life-giving, soul-reaching words Jesus spoke. They were everything I needed to hear. I had to grab hold of them and be present with them.

Sometimes you just have to take a moment. There will always be tasks to complete and work to do, but when the moment calls you, when God places you right in the face of an unexpected encounter or blessing, don't miss it. Sometimes we work so hard and get so focused on what we think is important that we ironically miss the most important thing. If I had done what I "should" have done that day, I would have missed the opportunity for Jesus to pour into my life and speak into my soul. I had to release myself from everyone's expectations and be free to receive what was mine. That was the biggest lesson I learned that day: not to be controlled by other people's plans and agendas for me. Rather, what I must focus on is what God has planned for me. Each day I need to pursue that question.

Be careful of that word "should"; it's often a trap. It enslaves you to others' expectations and keeps you from your ultimate goal.

If you want to know how to get this right each time, I'm not sure I know exactly, but I am sure it will mean quieting your spirit so you can hear from God. You'll know when you've made the right choice because you will receive a confirmation. Jesus did that for me when he told my sister that what I had chosen would not be taken from me. And I thank God for that because I had such an incredible soul-shaping moment with Jesus that day. It opened up parts of myself that enabled me to do crazy but powerful things later, like lovingly anoint him for his burial while he was still alive! That only happened because of that special time I had shared with him and the way I learned to listen to him. I had served him that day and several times after that, but in my own way.

So I encourage you to be yourself and lean into who you are, taking advantage of the special moments that God gives you, for you don't know when they'll appear again. Even if it disrupts your plans or others', you can't go wrong when you choose to be present to what God is doing in and for you. Block out anyone who doesn't understand. Don't let them distract you. The experience will be worth it. It will be transformative. It will be satisfying. It will be everything you need.

With hope and love,

—MARY

MORE LIKE MARTHA

Six days before the Passover, Jesus
came to Bethany, the home of Lazarus,
whom he had raised from the dead.
There they gave a dinner for him.
Martha served, and Lazarus was one of
those at the table with him.
∽ JOHN 12:1–2

It is a glorious moment, one overflowing with love, gratitude, and joy for everything they have just witnessed. Mary,
Martha, Lazarus, Jesus, and surely a large extension of family
and friends are enjoying a cookout. But this is no ordinary
family get-together, for they have all just witnessed a miracle: Lazarus was dead, and Jesus resurrected him. They saw
their deepest sorrow transformed into the greatest joy. Nat-
urally, it's time to celebrate, so they head to Lazarus's house
for dinner, where Mary famously washes Jesus's feet with
her hair.

Almost lost in the story, though, is Martha. All the chapter says about her is that she *served*. Why is that important? Why is this shared with us at all?

It could be that this very brief statement shows us a different, more at-peace Martha than the one in Luke 10:38–42 who couldn't believe her sister had the nerve to sit there being chatty at a previous gathering when she clearly needed help with all the cooking, cleaning, and serving. In Luke, she demanded that Jesus make her sister come assist her, but he defended Mary, suggesting that Martha look at the condition of her own spirit and the distracted, worried, and frantic internal space she'd created within herself.

But this time is different. It's almost the exact same story. Yet again, Martha is doing the work of hosting and serving dinner alone, and her sister is not helping. Rather, Mary is off doing the spiritual but seemingly unnecessary task of anointing Jesus while Martha serves. However, this time, Martha is not frantic or worried. She seems happy to serve and share. How did she get there? We can't be sure.

It's possible that in the scene in Luke, she forgot why she was being hospitable. Her preparations had become about the work, not about the people she was caring for. In this way, Martha reminds us to stay mindful of the deeper purpose of what we do and to walk in grace as we do it. Perhaps Jesus's remarks to her were the reality check she needed in order to realign with her own purpose. She had to embrace her reason for serving and lean into the joy that lived therein.

Further, she had to learn to stop expecting her sister to be like her. Martha was the one with the gift for hospitality; that was hers to share, not Mary's. The sooner we embrace our unique gifts as our own and do the same for others, the more peace and harmony we can create in our families and communities. Everyone has their own talents, abilities, and missions, and our families should be a place where we encourage everyone to pursue them authentically. When Martha does this, it creates space for Mary to do this incredible thing for Jesus, ultimately anointing him for burial. When we embrace who we are and love ourselves fully, we give ourselves and others the opportunity to flourish.

Please turn to the next page for a GUIDED REFLECTION. ≫→

69

GUIDED REFLECTION

Think about who you are. Proudly name your gifts, talents, passions, and abilities. Consider whether you embrace them and share them openly and authentically. Reflect on ways you can embrace them more.

WEEK 22

LISTENING FOR WHOLENESS

But the woman, knowing what had
happened to her, came in fear and
trembling, fell down before him, and
told him the whole truth.
∽ MARK 5:33

The woman described in Mark 5:25–34 couldn't remember
the last time she had actually felt good. The past 12 years
were a painful blur of bodily torture. Countless doctors, pay-
ments, and painful nights had not provided any relief. She was
still bleeding without any hope of healing, until finally Jesus
came to her town. This was her chance for healing, and she
knew it; she believed she could, so she did. As Jesus was on his
way to heal a little girl, she made her way through the crowd
determined just to touch him without being noticed. She slyly
maneuvered through the masses and grabbed his robe—and
then it happened. It was done. The bleeding stopped, and she
could go rebuild her life.

But Jesus paused and asked who had touched him, whose faith had called healing power out from him. He demanded that the person come forward. What was it like to be called out like that in front of everyone, no hiding allowed? What was it like to share with Jesus and her whole community the restoration she had experienced and tell her story about how her life had now changed? The text says the woman came forward, trembling and scared, and told him "the whole truth."

Imagine that. She told her whole truth, finally. After 12 years of pain, struggle, and isolation, she got to tell the secrets she had been holding in. What chapters were included in her story? And how long did it take? What did she say? Did she tell him about how intense her pain was? Or how hard it was being separated from family and friends? How she hadn't gotten married and couldn't bear children? We may never know what her "whole truth" entailed, but it doesn't matter what she said. What matters is that she finally got to say it. After holding it all in for more than a decade, she got to tell it all because Jesus had asked to be her listener.

Have you been there? Have you ever needed to let it all out? To tell the truth of all the chaos you've been through, the heaviness you've carried, the depression you've experienced? What did it feel like to be able to tell that truth, and how empowering and affirming was it that someone wanted to listen? Perhaps you still haven't been able to release your story. Maybe it's still pent up inside. But this woman's story shows us that Jesus wants to hear it. It's so important to him that he risked exposing her otherwise covert operation of touching the garment to be sure she had a chance to tell it. He knew she needed to release it for her healing to be complete.

If you've ever known the value of finally letting the pain pour out of you, then allow this story to be your model. You be the listener that welcomes someone to tell their whole truth. You may not be a therapist or a pastor, and you aren't expected to be Jesus, but showing someone that their story is valuable enough to be told is something we can all choose to do by simply listening. When the moment is ripe, welcome into the light those dark truths that are keeping others captive, isolated, and in pain. Cultivate spaces in your church, family, or friend group that champion this kind of truth-telling. Then point them to communal resources for healing, like therapy or counseling—but also to the One who can handle all the pain and transform their suffering into a powerful testimony.

THE CASE FOR QUIET

"Be still, and know that I am God! I
am exalted among the nations, I am
exalted in the earth."
∽ PSALM 46:10

We live in a loud, busy world. Even if we try to live simpler lives, our culture is constantly pushing us to produce, to listen in, to work, to do anything but be still or quiet. Even our rests are not restful, and people often return from vacation actually needing a vacation. We run ourselves ragged, promising ourselves that we'll cut back soon. We'll relax tomorrow. But then tomorrow comes, and we're off to the next thing. And if that isn't enough, life throws curveballs our way on a regular basis.

But in the midst of the chaos, we're called to stillness and quietness. It might sound ridiculous, but it is often the best possible response. The psalmist describes with vivid images just how out of control their life is in this moment, but they remind themselves to just be still and know God. Even if you only give it five minutes per day, make a point to get still and know that God is God, that truth has the power to calm the chaos and bring rest to our spirits. It will help remind you that if everything completely crumbles and disaster over-takes your whole world, God is still real. The only way to find the peace this knowledge brings is to regularly take a pause to remember it by being still, knowing that God is God.

I know this is a huge ask. If you're a mom, a wife, a friend, a leader, or a supporter of any kind, the last thing you probably feel like you have time to do is sit still. It can seem counterpro-ductive to stop and be still when we have a million things to do and not enough time to do them. But quiet time with God is the very thing that will nourish you for the busy times ahead. It may or may not make you more productive, but it will defi-nitely make you more yourself, more of who God created you to be. Embracing a practice of holy quietness will deepen your faith, strengthen your resolve, and revitalize your spirit. Trust God to take care of things while you step away for a moment to care for your own spirit.

Please turn to the next page for a JOURNAL PROMPT. ≫→

JOURNAL PROMPT

Spend some time thinking about the beauty and value of stillness and quietness. If being still is a challenge for you, it might be helpful to think about why. Are you a person who has a hard time sitting still when it seems like you should jump in and fix things? Do you feel that you always have to be doing something? Why is that? What would happen if you just tried to sit in your home in complete silence? What does that feel like? Moreover, why do you think we have been called to this? What might God be intending to teach or show us through a practice of stillness?

Now name your hesitation or objections to this practice and make a list. Why have you not embraced this as a practice before now?

Talk to friends and family about their thoughts on this. Do they practice stillness? What insights did you gain by speaking to them?

THAT SASSY SYROPHOENICIAN WOMAN

He said to her, "Let the children be fed first, for it is not fair to take the children's food and throw it to the dogs." But she answered him, "Sir, even the dogs under the table eat the children's crumbs." Then he said to her, "For saying that, you may go—the demon has left your daughter."
∞ MARK 7:27-29

Often identified as "the Canaanite woman" in Christian tradition, the Syrophoenician woman has one of the most intriguing encounters with Jesus in all of the Gospels. Her child has been afflicted with a demon, so when she hears that Jesus is in her neighborhood, she comes to him seeking a miracle. Strangely, though, Jesus hesitates—resists, even.

He says something about dogs, children, and who should eat first—apparently not her or her erratically behaving child. But she persists and delivers one sentence that changes everything, and when she returns home, she finds her daughter free from what had tormented her. As readers, we're happy that the healing happened, but we may also be a bit confused by this odd conversation.

The exchange between Jesus and the Syrophoenician woman is loaded with historical, social, and cultural baggage that creates a divide between the two of them. In Jesus's view, she is *other*—more specifically, "Greek" (i.e., a Gentile)—and Jews are the focus of his calling (Matthew 15:24), so the miracles he performs are not yet hers to have. But, unwilling to go away without what she came for, she argues back.

Womanist New Testament scholar Mitzi Smith beautifully identifies her words as "sass," a useful and powerful form of "talking back," especially as embodied by African American women. Our heroine is both Syrian and Phoenician, likely mixed race. Syrian Phoenicia had once been conquered by a group of Jewish rebels, although it was subsequently annexed back to Rome. But the sassy Syrophoenician doesn't waste her precious moments sorting out these heavy cultural, racial, and theological challenges with Jesus. Frankly, she doesn't have time for that; she has her child's wellness on her mind. Cleverly, she agrees with Jesus, using his own words as a strategy to win him over. It works!

But notice that Jesus emphasizes that her own words have healed her child. Her mouthiness, a characteristic often frowned upon in women, is what transforms her and her daughter's reality. There is real power in her words, which reframe the conflict, making Syrophoenicians partakers of food at the table, even if only receiving the crumbs the children drop.

This smart, strategic Syrophoenician got it done with the power of her words. There are several insights to gain from her actions. First, she was 100 percent focused on the matter at hand. She likely understood Jesus's hesitation to help her on the basis of her Greekness, but she didn't care. She was a mother with a suffering child, and that was her only focus. Whether she belonged there or not, she would do whatever she could to get her child relief. To her, *that* is what mattered most. It is so important that when we advocate for the lives of the suffering, we let them and their stories be the driving force of our movements, refusing to be stopped by obstacles in our way.

Moreover, she used her words so strategically here. She literally spoke her way into restoration. Her story asks a few questions of us: How can you use your words in ways that expand rather than constrict, that unlatch rather than lock down, that unveil rather than hide? Her mouthiness cut through the red tape and delivered a victory for her child. In this way, the sassy Syrophoenician woman models beautifully for us the wisdom of Proverbs 18:21: "Death and life are in the power of the tongue, and those who love it will eat its fruits." What kind of fruit will your words land on your table?

A HOPE AND A FUTURE

For thus says the Lord: Only when
Babylon's seventy years are completed
will I visit you, and I will fulfill to you
my promise and bring you back to
this place. For surely I know the plans
I have for you, says the Lord, plans for
your welfare and not for harm, to give
you a future with hope.
∽ JEREMIAH 29:10–11

Jeremiah 29:11 is a much-quoted scripture text and a favorite
in Christian circles. Its words are so encouraging that we find
them on mugs, greeting cards, and T-shirts. It's one of those
scriptures that gives us hope and makes us believe God really
does have our best interests at heart and has incredible blessings waiting for us just around the corner. While it's true that
the text essentially promises the people of Israel that God has
good things in store for them, we often completely skip over
the context of these words. The people of Israel have been

sent into exile in Babylon, not by their enemies but by God as punishment for their lack of faithfulness. One verse earlier, Jeremiah 29:10 clearly says that only after the Israelites have completed 70 years in exile will God visit them and fulfill the promise to return them home.

While we often share this message without thinking much about the context of the passage, if we look more closely at what's happening, it can be an even richer encouragement to the person of faith. Sometimes, like the people of Israel, we find ourselves in some pretty sticky situations. And yes, God does discipline us at times. It's not the most pleasant thing to think about, but there are times when we are forced to suffer the consequences of our actions. But this is when a text like Jeremiah is especially helpful to consider. Note this: God is telling the Israelites that they will be "on punishment" for 70 long years, but that it won't last forever. It will end at a certain time, and all of it will help secure their future. Despite what they've done and the consequences they'll now live through, God is still mindful of them and plans not to harm them but rather to give them a future and hope.

Think about a time in your life when you knew you'd done wrong. We often feel really low and bad about ourselves, possibly embarrassed. We may feel lonely, scared, insecure, or all of the above. But then also think about how encouraging it would be to know that this won't be the end of your story. That, despite your poor choices or your current predicament, God won't let it last forever. You will recover from this, and even better, God has a plan to secure a brighter future for you. There is a way in which this truth has the power to uplift our spirits, remove the heaviness we feel, and give us something to look forward to. While we may still have to stand through some consequences, we know that things will get better. And more than that, God has not given up on us, is still thinking about us, and is planning good for us.

Can you commit to revisiting this scripture the next time you find yourself in the midst of some painful situation that you know you caused? Encourage yourself and know that God still has a plan for you, to give you hope for the future.

JOURNAL PROMPT

Do some journaling about the last time you had to endure some not-so-pleasant consequences of your actions. Can you remember how you felt—embarrassed, worried, scared, ashamed? How might reflection on this text have been helpful to you at the time? How can you be grateful that this was God's promise to you then just as it is now? How does that make you feel?

WEEK 26

WHEN JESUS STANDS WITH YOU

The scribes and the Pharisees brought
a woman who had been caught in
adultery; and making her stand before
all of them, they said to him, "Teacher,
this woman was caught in the very act
of committing adultery. Now in the law
Moses commanded us to stone such
women. Now what do you say?"
∽ JOHN 8:3–5

There are so many places in scripture where God promises
to be with us in our challenges, and this story is an incredible
example of that. This woman had been caught committing
adultery, but the religious leaders were less concerned with
that and more concerned with testing Jesus to see how he'd
react. Would he encourage them to stone her, according
to the law? Or would he speak against the law and show his
typical compassion and care, disregarding her moral failures?

But Jesus was no fool. He knew they were trying to set him up and using this woman as a pawn to do so. And though she was probably terrified, she was actually in the best of possible circumstances. Standing with her was God made flesh, most powerful and most wise, who knew exactly how to defend her. In this story, we see that it is impossible to outsmart God. You will lose every time. Moreover, God won't allow our detractors to use our failings to pursue their wicked ends. At the end of the day, all have sinned and all are in need of a Savior.

Again, this woman's story, like so many in the Bible, isn't solely hers. She is caught in the middle of a conflict between Jesus and the religious leaders. She happened to be at the wrong place at the wrong time, and sometimes that lands us in pretty hot water. She was facing death by stoning, so the stakes couldn't have been higher for her. Imagine her standing there, shaking, crying, as she looked out at the crowd of people—some strangers, some people she knew—judging her. How must she have felt? Exposed, alone, humiliated. She never even gets to tell her side of the story. And, by the way, where was the person with whom she was cheating? Why was that person not subject to this public ridicule and attack? She had to stand there and take this all by herself.

Have you been there? Forced to take full responsibility for something others did *with* you? Called out in front of everyone? Maybe you were in the wrong, but an open attack in front of what feels like your whole world is heavy to take. But take your cues from this woman. Trust that God sees all and knows the way you are being treated and is able to step in to help you. Know this: You are not your mistakes. God sees not only what you've done but also who you are, your purpose, your future, and your light. And in God's eyes, you are worthy of compassion, mercy, and advocacy.

PART III

WEEK 27

SARAH AND ABRAHAM GIGGLED

Then Abraham fell on his face and
laughed, and said to himself, "Can
a child be born to a man who is a
hundred years old? Can Sarah, who is
ninety years old, bear a child?"
∾ GENESIS 17:17

So Sarah laughed to herself, saying,
"After I have grown old, and my
husband is old, shall I have pleasure?"
∾ GENESIS 18:12

Why did Sarah laugh? It's a question many have pondered.
But an equally valid question is why, in the study of this story,
have most focused exclusively on Sarah's laugh, ignoring
Abraham's? What's going on here? Did somebody get the
story wrong? Though this repetition is possibly an effect of the

pre-biblical oral tradition, the Bible says that *both* spouses laughed upon hearing the news that, at ages 100 and 90, they would be getting ready to bring a child into the world. Still, Sarah's is the one we remember and the one we revisit when exploring stories about faith, promises, and fulfillment.

Perhaps Sarah being a woman makes her giggle especially intriguing. After all, she's the one who will have to bear the child. She's also the one who, for at least 75 years, has had to wear the title of "barren" as a public badge of dishonor. In fact, when she's first introduced in scripture, that is how she is described: "Now Sarai was barren; she had no child" (Genesis 11:30). That's all we get. She has had to watch all the women around her bear children and raise them together, and she could not participate. She's so desperate to have a child that she even makes her husband marry her slave-girl, Hagar, so Hagar can produce an heir for her. This, of course, becomes a painful drama for everyone. In the end, Hagar and her child, Ishmael, leave, and Sarah's actions have all been in vain.

So much has happened and so much time has passed that she has likely given up on her desire for children. Perhaps that's reasonable, because at this point, she's old enough to have great-grandchildren. So when she hears this promise from God, she has to be in disbelief. She says to herself, "After I have grown old, shall I have pleasure?" *Will my dream actually come true?* She laughs to herself at the absurdity of it all.

Has this ever been you? So convinced that your time had passed, that it was too late to have the life you wanted, that you had actually given up on your dream? More than anything, this story asks us to examine the timelines that we subscribe to. Sarah's story suggests that the plots we fashion for our lives may not line up with our realities, and that's okay: Perhaps it's the timeline or plotline that needs to be abandoned, not our dream.

Second, Sarah's laugh could have had a variety of qualities. It could be rooted in cynicism, disbelief, joy, or even pain. But regardless of what's beneath it, her laugh represents a disruption in her assumptions about her life. This shows us that dream-chasing can sometimes be a long journey that can breed apathy and resignation if we allow it. If we're going to attain what we want, we have to be open to a disruption of our pain and disappointments. We have to allow for a new narrative to emerge.

Please turn to the next page for a GUIDED PRAYER. ≫→

GUIDED PRAYER

Think about something you've really wanted for a long time but can't seem to grasp. What is it? How do you feel about it? Where are you with it now? Still hopeful? Numb? Not sure? Angry? Disappointed? Resentful?

Now I challenge you to take those feelings and form them into a prayer:

"Lord, you know I have long desired

_____. I feel _____

that it hasn't happened. I give these feelings to you and ask for your blessing and guidance. Open my eyes to the possibilities I cannot see. Root me in love and trust in you. Amen."

SHARING JESUS

He came and took her by the hand
and lifted her up. Then the fever left
her, and she began to serve them.
∾ MARK 1:31

It was the Sabbath, and the disciples had all gathered at
Simon and Andrew's house after worship at the synagogue.
When they saw that Simon's mother-in-law had come down
with a fever and was lying in bed, they immediately told
Jesus about it. Then three things happened: Jesus came, she
was healed, and she began to serve. It's a brief story, but it's
jam-packed with encouragement for us.

First, it's critical to notice that the disciples had been
at the synagogue for worship, part of their typical routine
on the Sabbath. But what made this day special was that, at
the synagogue, they had seen Jesus take authority over an
unclean spirit and cast it out of a man (Mark 1:21–27). It was
an incredible experience for them, and their actions show that
they brought that experience out of the synagogue *with them*,

because when they got home and saw Simon's mother-in-law suffering, they immediately told Jesus.

The fact is, not everyone who needs help is coming into our churches. How can we allow experiences as the *gathered* community of God (corporate worship) to lead us into ministry that does good as the *scattered* community of God (at home, at work, in the community)? It's so easy to let our church experiences make us self-righteous or judgmental, but how can they make us helpful to those who need us? Of course, when Jesus arrives, he heals Simon's mother-in-law, and a situation that could have gotten much worse (fever was something to take even more seriously in a world before modern medicine) quickly becomes better.

But while this could be the end of the story, it isn't. After she gets up from the bed, Simon's mother-in-law serves Jesus. What's not obvious to an English reader is the way the Greek language captures this moment. The Bible says she serves them using the same word (*diakon*) it uses to describe the angels ministering to Jesus after his temptation in the wilderness (Mark 1:13). She performs a ministry. It's a blessing, divine and sacred work.

This is powerful. Now relieved of her illness, she can be a blessing to Jesus, extending care to him. And all this because the disciples shared their experience with Jesus with someone else who needed him. She was healed with a purpose. All those we encounter in our daily lives, who have problems, challenges, illnesses—they all have purpose, work, a calling. They are just as valuable as anyone. Simon's mother-in-law proves that to be true. Our task as believers is to faithfully share the love of Jesus and to witness to his power. It just might yield a healing, restoration, or deliverance for someone, freeing them for meaningful service to God.

AND THE STORM OBEYED HIM

They went to him and woke him up, shouting, "Master, Master, we are perishing!" And he woke up and rebuked the wind and the raging waves; they ceased, and there was a calm.

∞ LUKE 8:24

This is one of those very familiar stories of Jesus and his disciples in which Jesus reveals another aspect of his limitless power. They're out on a lake, trying to get from one side to the other in a boat, and while they're sailing, Jesus goes to sleep. But while he's sleeping, a strong storm arrives, and the boat begins to fill up with water and sink. Terrified for their lives, the disciples wake Jesus. Almost effortlessly, he rebukes the storm and it obeys him. He then asks, "Where is your faith?" (and probably goes back to sleep). Standing there in awe of what they've just seen, tears rolling down their faces, hearts still pounding, they ask each other what just happened. Had they really seen Jesus command the wind and the waves? And the elements obeyed? They were astonished, relieved, and in disbelief.

You may or may not have been caught without shelter in a thunderstorm, earthquake, hurricane, or tornado, but I'm sure you've lived through some spiritual storms. Those emotional downpours that scared you beyond belief were real to you. Like the disciples, you felt like Jesus was sleeping at the point of your deepest distress, and you cried out to him for help. These storms sometimes form quickly and barge onto the deck of your life; other times they can be seen a long way off, but somehow you still can't avoid them. They might involve trouble with your spouse or partner, children, friends, or job. It could be your health, or it could even be trouble in your mind. Sometimes it's nothing external at all. Sometimes the storms that rage are inside us, but Jesus speaks peace to those, too—and they obey him.

But this passage helps us understand how we ought to behave in the midst of the storm. We should notice that even though the disciples didn't know Jesus could control the weather, the reality was that he did and could always be trusted in the midst of the storm. We don't have to literally wake God up to see what chaos has broken out in our lives. God already knows, and whether God has moved yet or not, we can be sure that at any time, God *can* act to save us.

Moreover, Jesus demonstrates an incredible inner calm throughout the experience, modeling how the disciples should behave. Rather than screaming and running around in terror, perhaps they might have maintained their inner peace and simply trusted God to act if necessary. In the midst of a storm, our overly anxious behavior doesn't serve us well. It's an energy drainer. What would it mean if the next time a storm broke out in your life, you chose not to fall apart, not to worry yourself to death? Could you tap into your faith in a way that assured you that, no matter what happened, you would trust God and ride the storm out *with* God?

Jesus was in the boat, too. The disciples were not alone, and neither are you. How can you allow this truth to shape your next experience in a storm?

Please turn to the next page for a JOURNAL PROMPT. ≫→

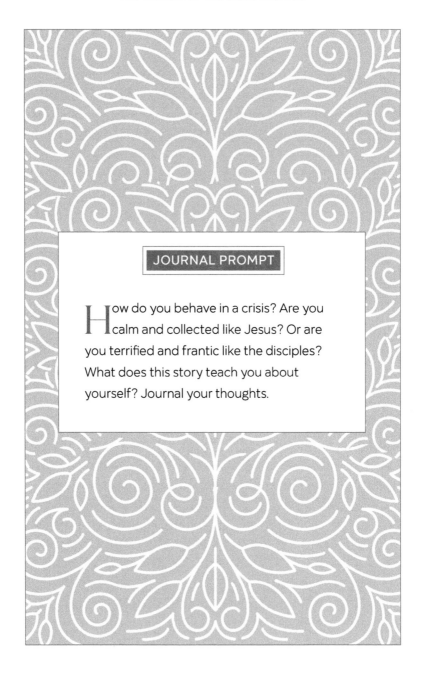

JOURNAL PROMPT

How do you behave in a crisis? Are you calm and collected like Jesus? Or are you terrified and frantic like the disciples? What does this story teach you about yourself? Journal your thoughts.

30

WHAT SHE SAW: MARY MAGDALENE AT THE CROSS

This was to fulfill what the scripture says, "They divided my clothes among themselves, and for my clothing they cast lots." And that is what the soldiers did. Meanwhile, standing near the cross of Jesus were his mother, and his mother's sister, Mary the wife of Clopas, and Mary Magdalene.
∽ JOHN 19:24–26

They had been everywhere together. She'd traveled with him as he spent endless days taking care of the sick, the hurting, the demon-possessed. (Mary Magdalene had been one of them herself, as he had cast out seven demons from her in Luke 8:2–3.) She had seen him work miracles in the lives of everyone they encountered. He'd changed her life, so she, along with many other women, committed to supporting him (Mark 15:40–41). Who knows how long she'd been journeying with him throughout his ministry, but it was long enough to know him—the real him.

As she stood at the foot of the cross, looking up at his dying, bloody figure, what might she have been thinking? As she looked back down at the guards casting lots to divide up his clothes, what was she feeling? This injustice was far too much. They were all wrong. He was innocent, a good man, and he didn't deserve this violent death at the hands of the state. But here they were. It was happening. And she couldn't do anything about it.

Throughout history, so many women have had to endure the sight of the ugliest, most heinous acts of violence, and just like Mary Magdalene, they were powerless to do anything about it. What does this kind of moment require from you? How does it shape you, or better yet, how can you shape yourself through it? How does Mary maintain her composure? If you've been where she was, if you've looked up and found that your worst fears have come true, Mary models how to make it through.

If nothing else, Mary was determined to be the true friend she had always been to Jesus, so she stayed until the end. Where else would she be? She had spent days traveling with and supporting him, and that day at Calvary was no different. If he was going to look down at the people below, he would not only see the Roman guards—he would also see the faces of loved ones who were loyal to him even in death. What would it mean for you to demonstrate this kind of love? It had to be horrible to watch, but she stayed and expressed ultimate devotion to the one who had transformed her life.

Moreover, Mary knew the truth of who Jesus was. She could stay there because she still believed in him. The lies the religious leaders had spread did not change what she knew to be true. Was he man? Was he God? She didn't know yet. What she knew was that he was no false prophet, and he had no plans to take over the government or challenge Roman authority. He was sent from God to do good in the world and show us how to live, and he had done that. She had watched him, over and over, transform people's lives for the better. The horrors of life can shake us to the core and stop us from seeing and being the good in the world. Evil is all around us, attempting to challenge our ethical framework and keep us from believing in God's power and love. But we have to hold on to our faith, no matter how ugly it gets. Mary fought back by simply standing still in the face of it and holding on to the truth. And so should we. Remember, the psalmist said that "weeping may endure for the night, but joy comes with the morning" (Psalm 30:5).

MARY'S JOY IN THE MORNING

Mary Magdalene went and announced
to the disciples, "I have seen the Lord";
and she told them that he had said
these things to her.

∾ JOHN 20:18

Ah! What joy awaited Mary Magdalene in the morning! If Calvary had been her worst fears and terror made real, then Sunday at the tomb was mourning turned to dancing. God had transformed the dark night into the brightest morning, both figuratively and literally. In a moment, everything had changed. Jesus had died, but he was now . . . alive again? That morning Mary woke up with the same pain and heaviness she'd been feeling for the past two days. It had really happened. They had killed Jesus, and for nothing. All she knew to do was to keep expressing her love and care as she always had. So she prepared the spices to go to the tomb and anoint his dead body. Except, of course, when she arrived, he was gone. Overcome with even more sorrow, she went to alert the others, but when she returned, she wept bitterly, sitting in the place where he had lain. Not only was he dead, but his body was missing. How could things get any worse?

But everything changed when Jesus appeared to her in the tomb and called her by name! Just like that, the nightmare was over. She cried out, *"Rabboni!"* ("Teacher!") when she saw the Lord, and nothing was the same.

Mary's experience is a reminder that things do get better. There is real joy that awaits us if we endure through the night. Now, "enduring through the night" does not mean anything abominable, like staying in an abusive relationship. It means refusing to let go of faith, regardless of what we experience. It means trusting that God will show up to transform, deliver, heal, comfort, set free, and restore. In fact, sometimes God does the best work when the challenges are the darkest.

Mary had remained faithful to her friend and held tightly to her beliefs in the midst of the worst times in life. She didn't buckle under social pressure or abandon her convictions when things started to look bad. That same faith is what led her to the tomb that morning to remain a devoted friend. That same resolve fostered her encounter with the risen Lord. She was the first to have that life-changing experience, and her faith situated her so that she could see it firsthand and run to tell others about it.

What deep experiences of faith might be shaping you for an encounter with the risen Lord? What challenges, if you just hold on, are preparing you to really see God? To both elevate and deepen your faith? So many don't make it to their resurrection experience because they give up when it gets hard. They settle. They stop believing. They let the evil of the world destroy their faith and bankrupt their hope. But if you follow Mary's example and just hold on, there's an empty tomb waiting for you! There's unspeakable joy just around the corner.

WEEK 32

SIS, TAKE A REST

The apostles gathered around Jesus, and told him all that they had done and taught. He said to them, "Come away to a deserted place all by yourselves and rest a while." For many were coming and going, and they had no leisure even to eat.

∾ MARK 6:30–31

It's no secret that the life of the average woman is pretty full. For centuries, women have worn multiple hats. We are often the glue, the energy, the driving force of our families, communities, and workplaces. We are the planners and executors of projects big and small. We run businesses, head families, support friends, care for elders, undergird spouses, love children, show support, hug the hurting, encourage the empty, sit with the suffering. We care for the sick and for aging parents. You name it, we do it. Well, except for the one thing we often neglect to do: take care of ourselves. The lives we live are beautiful when they express love and care for all those entrusted to us, but they can become disjointed, unanchored, even empty and lacking in purpose when we don't take time to rest.

In our present text, we find Jesus working to ensure that the disciples practice self-care and rest after a few days or weeks full of powerful and painful work in ministry. Jesus had sent them out and given them orders for how to show up in the world and make a difference. And they had. They'd been casting out demons, anointing and caring for the sick, and curing people of their diseases. But it had not all been beautiful. They had just returned from burying a dear friend and beloved mentor, John the Baptist, who had been murdered for nothing, his body desecrated, his legacy disregarded. Life had been high but also very low. And when they gathered around Jesus, you could feel their restlessness and anxiety. They were so worked up that they hadn't even eaten. Instead of talking to them about all that had happened and stirring the energy any further, Jesus took them away for rest and solitude.

How do you retreat? Do you know when your spirit just needs a rest? Are you tuned into yourself enough to know when you need to pull away and take care of yourself? And are you disciplined enough to do it? This text shows us the value of knowing when to stop. We don't have to be doing something all the time. Even God took a rest after six days of working hard to create the world. And if God took a rest, surely we need to as well. Jesus puts this belief into practice here by requiring his disciples to get away from all the bustle, disengaging momentarily. This time and space is needed for our sanity, for clarity, and for processing. How can we work through all our experiences, reflect on lessons learned, and

SIS, TAKE A REST

then prepare ourselves to take on more if we never stop in the first place? We're not wired to go nonstop. That is why Sabbath is a commandment and a practice God established from the beginning. Rest is not simply something we *should* do, it's something we need. It restores us, rejuvenates us, and helps us refocus.

Please turn to the next page for a JOURNAL PROMPT. ⟫➤

JOURNAL PROMPT

What are the signs that you need to take a rest? Do you get agitated easily? Does your heart beat fast? Are you less attentive? Clumsy? What does your body feel like? What is your emotional state? Write this out as a way of becoming aware and learning about yourself. Then make a list of 10 ways you can create retreat, with and without spending money.

WEEK 33

THE TRAILBLAZING DAUGHTERS OF ZELOPHEHAD

Then the daughters of Zelophehad
came forward . . . and they said. . . .
"Why should the name of our father be
taken away from his clan because he
had no son? Give to us a possession
among our father's brothers."
∾ NUMBERS 27:1–4

It's such a simple, profound truth, but Nancy D. Solomon
was absolutely right when she said, "You get in life what you
have the courage to ask for." Few exemplify this as strongly
as did Mahlah, Noah, Hoglah, Milcah, and Tirzah. They
were the only surviving heirs of their father, Zelophehad,
and when it was time to divide up the Promised Land among
the tribes of Israel, they were determined to get what was
theirs. The only trouble was that there was no precedent for

107

women owning land. We see this challenge play out in the book of Ruth (4:1–12). A woman owning much of anything on her own was basically unheard of, but these women dared to ask for the unthinkable and boldly presented their claim before Moses. Moses talked to God, who affirmed their position, and they were awarded their land.

This short story reads like a transcript from a small-claims court case in which the facts are clear and the judge can make a quick and fair choice. But this was no small case; it was a major victory for these women and for all the women who came after them. What can we learn from these pioneering women?

First, they teach us not to doubt ourselves. Sometimes you know in your heart what is right, what you deserve, or what you want, but you might be hesitant to say something. Perhaps the desire you're holding close to your heart is something that's never been done before, or maybe you've never seen it. So what? It might be uncomfortable to ask, but go for it anyway. Rather than coming up with all the reasons you shouldn't pursue your desire or dream, make a list of all the reasons you should. Go ahead. Ask for the raise. Seek the promotion. The answer may surprise you. (And if it turns out your desire isn't the right one, God will show that to you one way or another. Take the step of faith—just remain open to God's movement while doing so.)

Second, these sisters stuck together. There is strength in numbers, and because they were united in purpose and cause, there were no inheritance disputes for Moses to sort out among them. It made the case easy to handle. How can you partner with like-minded people to achieve your desired end? Who are some likely allies in your cause?

Ultimately, the daughters of Zelophehad model for us the importance of going for it, even if it's uncomfortable or unprecedented. Much of what we want in life can be ours, but sometimes we're required to ask for it. No one was going to voluntarily give them the land, especially since they were women. They had to ask. Moreover, their asking was a catalyst for a change in the law, which then permitted women to own property. That was a major win, not only for them but for the entire community. What big ask are you avoiding? What will it take for you to finally go for it? Remember that your courage in asking just might transform the possibilities for those who are coming behind you.

WEEK 34

THE PROMISE OF PEACE

Do not worry about anything, but in
everything by prayer and supplication
with thanksgiving let your requests
be made known to God. And the
peace of God, which surpasses all
understanding, will guard your hearts
and your minds in Christ Jesus.
∽ PHILIPPIANS 4:6–7

Life comes with a varied mix of experiences—highs, lows, and everything in between. It can be at once joyful and exhilarating but also deeply painful, worrisome, and scary. We have opportunities to learn and grow through all we experience, but the roller-coaster ride of life seems to work hard to rob us of our peace. And no matter what we go through, what we are learning, and how we are growing, it seems none of that is truly worthwhile if our inner world is chaotic, anxious, and rooted in worry. The Apostle Paul is well aware of this, and in his letter to the church at Philippi, which he founded and was nurturing into mature faith, he drops a gem that serves as a powerful method for attaining peace through prayer.

The first part is to decide not to worry. This can seem like ridiculous advice, especially when you're facing real, anxiety-inducing situations. But Paul offers an alternative: Instead of worrying, *pray*. In other words, tell God what you really need. Express how you really feel to the One who can help. What would it look like for you to turn your worries and stress into prayer? What if, instead of stating your worries as worries, you reframed them as concerns lifted to God? This is not just empty talk; it is choosing faith over fear. It is offering your stress to God, who is happy to hold it and handle it for you.

The second step is to give thanks in the prayer. Gratitude elevates us above our challenges, allowing us to transcend them. It helps us refocus and reflect on the awesomeness and power of God. Moreover, gratitude (what Paul calls "thanksgiving") also humbles us because it has us acknowledge that someone else—in this case, God—is helping us, that we have not made it to where we are on our own.

Notice that through this formula we are now combining our worries (reframed into prayer) with our practice of gratitude, giving them both to God for safekeeping. Faith transforms the worries into prayer, and the gratitude then enriches the prayer *and us* with humility so that the prayer is offered in the right spirit. And we turn all of this into an offering that we give back to God, who gladly receives that gift from us and gives us peace in exchange.

Had you ever imagined that in order to receive God's peace all you had to do was humbly and openly give God the stuff that was robbing you of that peace in the first place? This does not mean that the problem goes away, but it does mean that the problem no longer has to control us, our attitude, our state of mind, or our temperament. This prayer is the key that unlocks the promise of God's peace for the believer. We can never stop all the anxiety-producing moments that life presents to us, but we can reach for and receive God's peace to face them when it does.

WEEPING WITH MICHAL

> Now Saul's daughter Michal loved David. Saul was told, and the thing pleased him. Saul thought, "Let me give her to him that she may be a snare for him and that the hand of the Philistines may be against him."
> ∽ 1 SAMUEL 18:20–21

Michal was in love. She thought David was attractive, strong, brave, honest, and smart. She saw him and wanted him, despite the fact the he was the target of her father Saul's foolish jealousy. For years, Saul had plotted to kill David, but that didn't matter to Michal. She loved David and was willing to risk her life to protect him. She even lied to her father twice to keep David safe (1 Samuel 19:10–17). No place else in the Bible does scripture proclaim that a woman loved a man (except in Song of Solomon, but the Shulamite woman is more a poetic figure than a historical person). This week's verse leaps off the page.

Michal married David, and like any other young bride, she hoped for a bright future and lasting love.

It's great to be in that happy, hopeful place we experience when we're in love. But sometimes it gets complicated, and in Michal's case, it was complicated from the start. She had only been allowed to marry David as part of a larger political scheme of Saul's. And even after she saved David's life, he had to leave to avoid Saul's murderous plot. Moreover, the text doesn't tell us that David ever loved her back. And if that wasn't enough, during David's years away, she is given in marriage to another man (1 Samuel 25:44). Her new husband, Palti, definitely loves her, but David eventually takes her back from him (2 Samuel 3:13–16). Michal finds herself back with the man she'd once loved so much, but everything has changed.

We've all been Michal in one way or another. There's nothing better than being in love, but it's no fun being there alone. Marriages in Michal's day were often about politics, land, power, and wealth, and as the king's daughter, she had to know that. But love always makes us believe that the impossible is possible. It matters that the text says Michal was in love with David, just like it matters so much to us when we choose to love. We go after what we desire, sometimes risking everything, as Michal did. And sometimes our hopes go unfulfilled. None of what happened was Michal's fault. All she had done was open herself to love.

Love sometimes ends in disappointment. Breakups happen. Children let us down. Parents sometimes abandon us. Relationships, plans, and dreams sometimes fold under the pressure they carry. Often it isn't even our fault, but we still have the task of trying to stitch our life back together in the aftermath. Michal represents everyone who has loved and hoped for something awesome but came up short. And it's important that we grieve for what happened to us—and what didn't. We have to be honest about what we lost and what we never gained. The next time that stuff surfaces, don't push it back down. Set it free. Release it to the wind and carry it no more.

Please turn to the next page for a JOURNAL PROMPT. ⟫→

JOURNAL PROMPT

If you're willing, write a journal entry about a love you lost, a relationship that ended, or some other hope that was dashed. What was the joy it brought you initially? What was the pain of not being able to hold it? Who made you angry in the midst of it? Write it all down and get it out. You're not necessarily looking for an answer or anything that makes it better. The goal here is to acknowledge your story, tell it and own it, and then release it.

MICHAL'S SIDE OF THE STORY

"I will make myself yet more contemptible than this, and I will be abased in my own eyes; but by the maids of whom you have spoken, by them I shall be held in honor." And Michal the daughter of Saul had no child to the day of her death.
∽ 2 SAMUEL 6:22–23

In 2 Samuel, we see a fight, a particularly ugly argument between a married couple: David and Michal. As described in last week's devotion, their story started out with a powerful love growing in Michal, but by this time, they couldn't be further from each other in understanding, intimacy, and partnership.

It is perhaps the most successful day of David's career. He has been fighting the Philistines since he was literally a teenager. Now a full-grown man, he finally secures a major victory by winning back what might have been Israel's most prized possession: the Ark of the Covenant. The Ark represented God's presence with Israel, and their enemies stole it—but David has recovered it! It's a mighty day in Israel's history. David probably isn't expecting to argue with his wife when he gets home, but Michal is ready to call him out for his supposed improper behavior—dancing in celebration while wearing only a linen undergarment—and she does just that.

But why? Michal shared the same faith as David. The meaning of this moment was not lost on her. What Israelite wasn't joyous and grateful that King David had brought the Ark back home?

All this implies that Michal wasn't really upset about David's bold worship. Wilda C. Gafney suggests in *Womanist Midrash: A Reintroduction to the Women of the Torah and the Throne* that, actually, Michal was hurt from having been abandoned by David—and, I would add, by her father as well. Remember, she loved David deeply, but he had to leave for years because of the bounty her father placed on his head. And then, when she finally did land with a new husband, David came back and snatched her away. Her new husband, Palti, publicly sobbed for her, revealing his great heartbreak. In all of this, Michal is being moved around like a pawn in everyone else's schemes.

Now she's back in the royal house, that same place that has controlled much of her life, and David has several other wives and children. He likely doesn't want to connect with her because she's been with another man, who clearly loved her. As the king, David may have felt he had to take her back for appearance's sake, but did he really want her? That's questionable. So in this text we see this couple, who have so much history weighing down on this moment. Even if Michal wanted to be happy for David, she couldn't. She looks at him and sees a man who could never love her. He looks at her and sees a woman he can never love. Too much has happened, and they can't start over.

Michal had no choice but to live with her new reality, but you can make choices that are better for you. This moment points to what happens when we refuse to have the critical conversations we should. What if David and Michal had laid it all on the table and shared how they really felt? What if David had said he didn't know if he could trust the love she had for him because of her father's schemes? What if she told him it hurt her that she risked everything to save his life but he hadn't returned that love? What if they had gotten vulnerable and told each other their truths? We have to learn to say the things we're scared to say so we can get to the source of our frustration and pain. Many times, we fight about the surface things that don't really matter and leave the real restorative work undone.

What difficult conversations are you avoiding? What fears are you covering up and not letting out? No relationship can sustain this kind of hiding. Unbury the truths you're holding within. It may not mend the relationship, but it will set you free from holding the pain of it.

WEEK 37

SAD NO MORE

And she said, "Let your servant find favor in your sight." Then the woman went to her quarters, ate and drank with her husband, and her countenance was sad no longer.
∽ 1 SAMUEL 1:18

Hannah had it hard. She lived in a world where a woman's worth was constantly measured by her ability to bear children, sons especially, and the text says that "[t]he Lord had closed [her] womb" (1 Samuel 1:6). She probably could have endured it if it hadn't been for Peninnah. The two of these women were in a polygamous marriage to Elkanah, and Peninnah had borne many children to her husband. She thought pretty highly of herself—so much so that she tormented Hannah about her "closed womb" every chance she got. Elkanah looked on Hannah with compassion as if he understood her suffering, desiring to be all that she wanted and more (1 Samuel 1:8). But she still needed to confront the root of her pain with the only One who could transform her situation: God.

So Hannah did just that. She took all the pain in her heart—the years of embarrassment, the feeling of unworthiness, the anger she felt at her own body—and she poured it out in a powerful prayer at the temple. And the thing that made the prayer powerful was that at its core was vulnerability, power-lessness, and humility laid bare before God. Hannah let the tears flow and the sobs hang heavy and uncomfortably in the air. This was her temple worship. It wasn't proper. It wasn't pretty. It was wild, unkempt, raw, and ugly. She had really taken all that she could. This was not the same trip to the temple she'd made in previous years. She decided that this time she would come back different, because this time, her worship, her prayer, was different.

And it worked. Regardless of what the outcome would be—child or no child—she had opened her heart and poured out all the pain to God. It was hers to bear no more. After this kind of transformative worship, she went home and ate well with her husband, reclined in his arms, and felt sad no more.

Hannah ultimately did get pregnant and gave birth to Samuel, one of Israel's greatest prophets, but she found her peace long before that. She got her relief before she got her answer. But how did she do that? And how can we do the same? I believe she got her relief because she finally faced her fears. She knew she hadn't been able to have children, but she hadn't spoken to God about it. Sometimes we wrestle with things too long because we're scared to actually con-front the fear that sits under them. We refuse to pray about some things precisely because we know God *will* answer us, and what if it isn't the answer we want? In this way, prayer makes us acknowledge that we aren't in control, forcing us to release the outcome back to God. That's why it was easier for Hannah to just take Peninnah's taunting all those years, though it was brutal. It was a kind of faux protection from the truth she was scared to hear.

What we learn from Hannah, then, is to ask the questions we most want answered, even when we're scared. Hannah's willingness to trust God's answer was what finally afforded her the peace she wanted. The same can be true for you. Your peace waits on the other side of your honest outpouring to God. Rather than wrestling alone with what you cannot control, why not ask God for what you need, trusting that if the outcome is not what you preferred, it is still for the best?

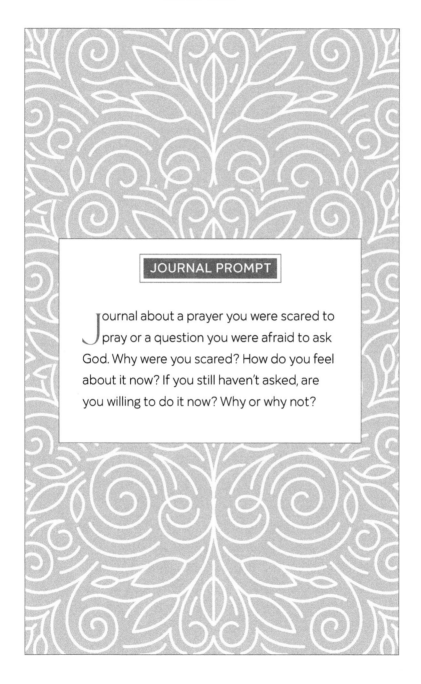

JOURNAL PROMPT

Journal about a prayer you were scared to pray or a question you were afraid to ask God. Why were you scared? How do you feel about it now? If you still haven't asked, are you willing to do it now? Why or why not?

A SACRED TRUST:
SAMSON AND DELILAH

When Delilah realized that he had
told her his whole secret, she sent
and called the lords of the Philistines,
saying, "This time come up, for he has
told his whole secret to me."
~ JUDGES 16:18

Samson, the last of the judges in the book of Judges, was
the strongest man in the world, and he made a habit of tor-
menting the Israelites' enemies, the Philistines. He was
powerful and apparently unbeatable in a fight. But he had
at least one weakness, and that was his love for Delilah. The
Philistine leaders, frustrated by his constant victories over
them, bribed Delilah to help them finally take him down. Her
task was simple: find out the source of Samson's strength.
Three times she asked him to tell her his secret, but each
time he lied, and each time she showed her true desire to take
away his strength by doing the thing he said would make him

weak. Still, after she protested enough, he finally told her the real truth: He would lose his strength if his hair were cut. Of course, she cut his hair, and the Philistines captured him, blinded him, and put him to work in a grain mill. They finally had him subdued, in part because Delilah was willing to help them do it. But why?

It is very clear in reading this story that it is Samson's story, not Delilah's; it's about Samson's dominance over the Philistines and their desire to get back at him. But locked away in the narrative stands this woman, Delilah, whom we don't know much about. Many assume she's a Philistine, but the text doesn't reference her nationality or ethnicity at all. All we know is that Samson is in love with her (Judges 16:4). And that makes her valuable to the Philistines who wish to finally subdue him. None of these circumstances that surround her actually have anything to do with her, but they still necessarily place her at the heart of a massive conflict between the Philistines and the Israelites. She ultimately has to decide where to place her loyalties: with him, the Philistines, or herself. Which does she choose, and why?

Love can lead us to do stupid things, and there is probably no better proof of that than Samson's choice to reveal the true secret of his strength to Delilah. What we don't know is why Delilah decided to exploit Samson's trust. Was it just to get paid? Did she have some financial burden of which we're not aware? Does she simply not love him the way he loves her? Did she feel she couldn't say no to the Philistine chiefs, who represented her society's power structure? We can't be entirely sure what motivated her to get on board with their plot, because she never gets to tell us. All we know is that she did it.

What we *can* do is reserve our judgment of Delilah and turn our attention to ourselves, allowing her story to guide us in careful reflection on our own motives and aims. What do *we* do when we're given the gift of someone's trust? Do we cherish it? Are we grateful? Do we protect it? Or do we access it for our own purposes and miss the sanctity of the moment? Perhaps no one is revealing some deep dark secret to you, but they might do you the honor of showing their real self, of taking the risk to be vulnerable. How will you choose to respond?

What if, instead of actually selling him out to the Philistines, Delilah, once Samson revealed his secret, told him hers? That's relationship. That's real intimacy. That's real humanity. That's love. It's the thing we all hope is possible: that we can show the real us and be loved and cared for, protected even. How will you fulfill that hope in your relationships?

WEEK 39

RAHAB'S INSIDE JOB

"Now then, since I have dealt kindly
with you, swear to me by the Lord
that you in turn will deal kindly with
my family. Give me a sign of good
faith that you will spare my father and
mother, my brothers and sisters, and
all who belong to them, and deliver our
lives from death."
∾ JOSHUA 2:12–13

Rahab is quite an impressive biblical character. She is a Canaanite woman who is celebrated in Christian scripture for her faith (Hebrews 11:31, James 2:25) and even gives birth to Boaz, which makes her the great-great-grandmother of King David and therefore an ancestor to Jesus (Matthew 1:5–16). Rahab is connected to greatness for sure. However, she also achieves greatness in her own right, so it might be better to say that greatness flowed from her.

Rahab lived in the city of Jericho around the time the people of Israel were coming to finally conquer their land. Rahab was a sex worker whose home was built into the city wall, which made it the perfect place for Israelite spies to hide when they came to scout out the land. She had a sense that Canaanite officials would come looking for those spies, so she hid them on her roof and lied about their whereabouts (Joshua 2:3–7). And then came her shining moment: She cut a deal with these spies. Since she spared them and risked her life by hiding them, they would spare her and all her family when they returned to take over Jericho. The spies were happy to oblige, and just like that, Rahab outsmarted the powers that be in Jericho, aligned herself with the winning side, and secured her family's future.

It's easy to overlook the gravity of her actions, but this was no small feat for a single woman in her day. She aided and abetted criminals, lied to the state, and committed treason. These kinds of offenses would surely land her in prison, even in contemporary times, but Rahab went for it anyway. Why? Because it was clear to her that the God of Israel was real. God's parting of the Red Sea, among other things, had made her believe (Joshua 2:10). Because of her courage, she and her family were spared.

Rahab teaches us the value of staying socially conscious of the world around us. She would not have even been aware of who the spies were or what their people had experienced had she not kept herself abreast of history and current events. That knowledge made her alert and aware of what was happening. So when the spies showed up, she knew why they were there—not for sexual pleasure but for a much more important task. She trusted her intuition and acted to protect them. She bet on the winning team, and it paid off.

How engaged are you in world affairs? How knowledgeable are you about history, politics, and the movements of governments and religious and other institutions? Are you paying attention? We are called to be much more than churchgoers and worshippers. We are called to be wise, courageous, and ready to act for good when we can. What might you learn from what you observe, and how might your faith motivate you to act when the time is right? Are you paying attention to the movement of God? How can you discern what's happening and what your place is in all of it? Maybe you aren't called to save your family but rather another group of vulnerable people who need your help. How does Rahab's story inspire you to stay informed and be courageous enough to act?

PART IV

NOT WITHOUT MIRIAM

So Miriam was shut out of the camp
for seven days; and the people did not
set out on the march until Miriam had
been brought in again.
~ NUMBERS 12:15

In today's scripture, the people of Israel are on their journey to their Promised Land. For 40 years, they have pressed on through the wilderness, carrying all they own and love, following their leader, Moses. Moses's work was challenging, trying to herd these people over many miles, listening to their complaints, keeping them focused.

But Moses wasn't alone. He had a sister named Miriam, who was a leader and prophet in her own right. In fact, she is understood in Jewish and Christian traditions to be the first woman prophet. Women clergy everywhere owe much respect to her as a leader of God's people. She was not only part of Moses and Aaron's ministerial team, she was also their big sister, who'd courageously acted to save Moses's

THE WOMEN OF THE BIBLE AND YOU

life and keep their family together when he was just a baby (Exodus 2:1–7). She also led the people in worship and dance as they made their way out of Egypt and through the Red Sea on dry ground, which was considered prophetic work (Exodus 15:20–21).

So what is happening in this week's verse? Why has she been shut out of the camp? In brief, Miriam and Aaron spoke out against Moses, likely in response to his choice to marry a foreign woman. Challenging his authority as the sole messenger of God, Miriam points out that God also speaks through her and Aaron (Numbers 12:2). God hears it and reprimands both of them. Miriam is struck with a horrible skin disease and forced to stay outside the camp for seven days. But, intriguingly, the whole camp refuses to leave her and waits until she is restored before moving forward. What can we make of all this? How is it helpful to us today?

Many scholars appropriately read Miriam's action in the context of Moses taking a new wife. This likely also means Moses had divorced his previous wife, Zipporah (Exodus 18:2), whom Miriam knew and perhaps loved. But this story isn't simply about a wedding. While Miriam may have been entitled to her feelings about Moses's marriage, her thoughts were better left unsaid precisely *because* she was a leader. If she spoke negatively about Moses, others would follow. This reveals a lesson: We must be mindful of how we use our influence, especially when we're in leadership roles. It's a sacred thing to handle people's hearts; it comes with great responsibility and should be approached with great care. Miriam could do great damage to the community, undermine their respect for Moses's authority, and threaten their mission of making it to the Promised Land.

Moreover, despite Miriam's frustration with Moses's choice, Moses was still *God's* choice, and that must be respected. Perhaps he *was* wrong to have left Zipporah, but it wasn't Miriam's place to challenge that, certainly not in the way she did. Sometimes we disagree with our leaders, but there's a way to engage in healthy dialogue about what we're feeling.

Like Miriam, we must learn that the eyes and ears of God are everywhere. In the heat of her rant, she's not thinking about this at all, but the text says, "And God heard it." A position of power does not push us beyond the reach of God. God is everywhere and sees and hears everything. When we fail to demonstrate that we know that, we may find ourselves shut out of circles of influence for a season (or longer).

Ultimately, there is some redemption for Miriam. Despite her misstep, she is restored to the community after being reminded of the power of her influence and how she must be more responsible with it. Her people added more days to their trip so they could wait out the punishment with her. Thank God we can recover and move past our mistakes and be remembered for who we are, not simply what we've done.

Please turn to the next page for a GUIDED REFLECTION. ⋙→

GUIDED REFLECTION

Spend some time reflecting on the influence you have on the people around you. Who listens to you? Who looks to you for guidance and leadership? Do you think of them when you make your choices? Are you responsible with your influence?

EMBRACING GRATITUDE

Give thanks in all circumstances; for
this is the will of God in Christ Jesus
for you.
∽ 1 THESSALONIANS 5:18

In this short but critical verse, Paul advises us to simply "give thanks" in all circumstances. While it seems like good advice and easy enough to follow, a moment of reflection on the difficulties of life might raise some questions. Are we expected to give thanks while we're in pain? When we're burying a loved one? Are we supposed to give thanks when friends betray us? What about when we're heartbroken, broke, stressed, or fearful? The Apostle Paul replies, "Yes, in every circumstance."

How dare he! The pain we feel in the darkest moments doesn't lend itself to gratitude. Who wants to be grateful for the things that break our hearts? But that's why we should be clear that the challenge posed to us is to give thanks *in* everything, not *for* everything. We're not asked to be grateful that something horrible has happened; that would be unfair. Rather, we're asked to be grateful to God in spite of what happened.

Why is this important? Giving thanks in the midst of dark times does at least three things: (1) It shifts our focus from our problem to the source of our power, reassuring us of God's presence and ability to help us; (2) it welcomes the light of God into the dark place, which warms our hearts and brightens our way; (3) it does inner transformative work that relieves our stress, elevating us above the difficulties. The pains of life oppress and depress us. They work to keep us down emotionally, physically, and psychologically, and all of that can be draining and immobilizing.

But when we shift our minds to gratitude, it revives the spirit and gets us moving again. This is because gratitude expresses the goodness and faithfulness of God; it's a reflection on the way God illuminates, activates, and animates our lives. It is a choice to focus on the positive and to respond in kind with words of praise and thanksgiving. That act reminds us of who God is, what God has done, and what God can do. All this focus on God brings warmth and light to spaces that felt cold and dark; it makes us feel better. And if we practice gratitude enough, it will work inside us and begin to heal some of the hurt places. All of this allows us to transcend our circumstances, rise above the mundane challenges we face, and commune with God. That frees us from the stress and the powerful hold our difficulties have on us.

I challenge you to practice gratitude the next time you're going through something painful. Remember, you don't necessarily give God thanks *for* what happens, but *in the midst of* what happens. If you're low on cash, thank God for being your provider. If someone you love dies, thank God for being your comfort. If you're feeling lost and confused, thank God for being your guide and protector. Rather than complaining about what's wrong, how can you embrace gratitude and the promise of who God can be for you?

MADE ON PURPOSE

"Before I formed you in the womb I
knew you, and before you were born
I consecrated you; I appointed you a
prophet to the nations."
∾ JEREMIAH 1:5

You were always wanted. You were always loved. You always
had purpose.

These famous words of Jeremiah 1:5 form part of the
prophet Jeremiah's call story. And call stories were a big deal
in his time. They served as a sort of credential, qualifying
the prophet to do their work. In this call story, God makes
clear that Jeremiah was always intended to be a prophet.
In fact, God handpicked him for the job. It even goes so far
as to say that God knew Jeremiah before he was conceived
in his mother's womb. All of this together created the evidence that Jeremiah was indeed called to serve as a prophet
to God's people. No question about it—he had been assigned,
equipped, created for the work.

The same is true for each of us. God knew you intimately before you had even been conceptualized in anyone's mind. You were no accident. You were meant to be here. And you made it here because God wanted you here. God loved you already and had something important for you to do. So whenever you start to feel unworthy, not valuable, not beautiful, not wanted, come back to this verse. God thought of you before creating you. The God of the universe envisioned you and then got busy making you. You originated in the mind of God. You are breathing because the most powerful and loving One desired it so. Let that sink in. It's your job to never forget that and to live that as your personal truth.

One caveat to keep in mind is that *God* made you for a divine purpose. People around us can try to project their own ideas and agendas onto us and call it divine. This can be true for any person, but it can show up in interesting ways for women. Women can often play many roles in our communities simultaneously: mother, wife, friend, sister, aunt, leader, supporter, church worker, etc. These are all beautiful roles that we often enjoy, but if we are not discerning and clear about what *God* has called us to, then we can find ourselves pursuing roles that never belonged to us. All this interaction can have us feeling obligated to make people happy instead of listening for God's guidance. The busier we are, the harder it is to hear. This is why it is vital that we constantly look to God for clarity on our purpose. To be sure, those answers may come through other people. Just practice tuning your spiritual ears to God's voice, and pray to be able to hear that above the noise.

You were always wanted by God. You were always loved by God. You always had purpose in God. Seek that out. Then go live it.

Please turn to the next page for a GUIDED REFLECTION. ≫→

139

GUIDED REFLECTION

Sit still for a while and reflect on this scripture. What comes up for you? Have you ever questioned your life's purpose or meaning? Have there ever been moments or experiences that made you feel unwanted? Name those experiences and write them down. What feelings do you have? What worries or fears do you have? How does this text help combat any negative thoughts?

Conversely, if you've always thought of yourself as full of purpose, what people, places, or events made you believe that? Name them, describe them, and give thanks.

If you had to put Jeremiah 1:5 into words that a 10-year-old could understand, how would you say it? Rewrite the verse as if you are sharing it with a child. Take your time, and explain it and write it well. Now read it to yourself aloud, pretending you're talking to 10-year-old you.

LET HER BE PRAISED

Charm is deceitful, and beauty is vain,
but a woman who fears the Lord is to
be praised. Give her a share in the fruit
of her hands, and let her works praise
her in the city gates.
∽ PROVERBS 31:30–31

This is one of the most treasured and controversial passages in the Bible when it comes to its discussion of women, our roles, our lives, and our place in the world—especially in our families. While some communities embrace the description of the woman in Proverbs 31:10–31 as both inspirational and aspirational, others find it unattainable. The Proverbs 31 woman is impressive and extraordinarily busy. She is a wife, a mother, and an astute businesswoman (31:16, 24), and amazingly, fulfilling any of these roles doesn't make any of the others any harder.

For example, her husband trusts her completely, she always treats him well (31:11–12), and she always makes him

THE WOMEN OF THE BIBLE AND YOU

look good in public (31:23). An excellent mother, she takes good care of her entire household, preparing everyone to face the outside world (31:21, 27), and she dresses well while doing so (31:22). Her husband and children praise her for her hard work (31:28). She gives help to others (31:20), she embraces wisdom and is apt to teach (31:26), and she is an extremely hard worker in all her enterprises, not hesitating to literally burn the midnight oil if need be (31:18–19). While many of us will read this and see our moms, grandmothers, godmothers, and aunts, whom we may adore and praise, an equal number of us will read this and feel overwhelmed.

While we sometimes feel fabulous because we've been productive, helpful, generous, and loving to those around us, there are probably more times when we feel we're anything but that. We may feel exhausted, like we're barely keeping up with life. We might have been caught on more than one occasion looking like a complete mess. And if we do manage to get the kids ready and make our spouses look good in public, when do we have time to pursue our own interests or do community service?

What can we do with those feelings of inadequacy? When we feel like we're crawling toward the finish line rather than sprinting past it? Embrace it, all of it: the good days and the bad, the struggle and the triumph. Embrace it all as your own glorious story, worthy of praise.

The woman depicted in Proverbs 31 is just that: a depiction. She's not a real person. She's an idea. But what if she were real? If she could speak for herself, what would she say? Would she describe herself like the writer of this proverb? Maybe, if she was feeling especially confident that day. But she might also mention the huge fight she had with her spouse or the time she missed a meeting with a potential investor because her kid was sick. It could be that she'd open up to us about all the times she felt empty and wanted to quit. She might give us the scoop on who she really was, how she really felt, and how things really went down. It would include all the fabulousness we read in the text but also all the rawness we know goes with it. We know this because we are her: the beautiful depiction we read and all the fleshy humanity behind it.

Sometimes our lives look and feel like those beautiful verses in Mother's Day cards, but other times, not so much. Though we sometimes make it look easy, we know it's often hard. Let our focus be on doing the best we can with what has been given to us. If it comes with some praise occasionally, enjoy that, too. You deserve it. But may you always yearn to serve and love God. And as you succeed and fail, struggle and triumph, know that there are millions of women cheering you on, and we are all right there with you, trying to do the same.

MARRIAGE, VIRTUE, AND WOMANHOOD

Who can find a virtuous wife? For her
worth is far above rubies.
∾ PROVERBS 31:10 (NKJV)

Virtuous womanhood: It's the theme for so many songs and sermons about Christian women. But is this a passage written truly for every woman? The woman in Proverbs 31 is wise, strong, committed to those she loves, crafty, creative, and successful in business. In other words, she's a boss. But must she be married and a mom? Are moms and wives the only women capable of virtue? What about women who aren't married yet? Or women who don't desire marriage or children at all? If you happen to be reading this passage as a single woman or reflecting back on your time as a single woman, what does this description of virtuous womanhood have to offer you?

First, it's helpful to note that the Hebrew word often translated into English as "wife" in this passage is *ishah*, which means both "wife" and "woman." It is likely that within the ancient Hebrew cultural context, there wasn't a huge distinction between the two. That, of course, is not the case for women today. We may find ourselves never married, divorced, widowed, single, "it's complicated," dating but not committed, or in any number of other relationship categories. But we need not think that any of those complexities keep us from the possibility of virtue, success, or the complete and full life described in Proverbs 31. And if we translate the word *ishah* as "woman," perhaps we can find ourselves more easily in the text.

Moreover, it might be valuable to consider this passage not as a biographical description but rather as a poem dedicated to many women. Perhaps it's not about just one woman's story but about many of our stories. It grasps the essence and spirit of how many of us live out our womanhood. Some of us are amazing in business. Some of us are great caregivers for children—even if we didn't give birth to any. Some women are crafty and artistic, while others are great as managers and leaders. This passage has so much to say about who we are and who we're striving to be. There's no need to let the common interpretation of "wife" limit the possibilities here. I challenge you to think more expansively about this text and find yourself in it. Find the inspiration. Better yet—be the inspiration.

Please turn to the next page for a SCRIPTURE STUDY. ≫→

SCRIPTURE STUDY

Take a few lines or verses of this passage (Proverbs 31:10–31). You don't need to try to tackle the whole passage, just the few verses that speak to you most. Your task is to rewrite them with yourself in mind. This is actually an old spiritual practice called "paraphrasing the Psalms," but it need not be psalms that you paraphrase. Feel free to recreate the story using yourself. Reflect on what you write and then go live it!

MY LIGHT

The Lord is my light and my salvation;
whom shall I fear? The Lord is the
stronghold of my life; of whom shall I
be afraid?
∽ PSALM 27:1

In week 29, we explored the merits of remaining calm in the midst of a crisis or challenging experience. Psalm 27 explains more about how we can achieve that. Considered a lament, this psalm finds the psalmist in the midst of an all-out war or attack on their life. Evildoers devour their flesh, and even an army encamps against them, lying in wait to make their strike. But throughout it all, the writer proclaims in one way or another that they will not let fear control them. How can the writer be so at peace when it feels like a whole army is waiting to take their life? Two things.

First, the writer proclaims that God is their light and salvation, so they have no reason to fear anything. This understanding that the God of the universe is on your side—is present to help, love, and protect you—can provide a sweet relief from the stress. If you know that God's light can brighten your path and cast out the darkness that has overcome you, you have nothing to fear. Moreover, God is the psalmist's salvation. So it doesn't matter what the chaos is. If needed, God is capable of rescuing them. Ultimately, this is all an example of the writer reminding themselves of what they know to be true. Moreover, the psalmist, instead of getting stressed, reminds themselves of who God is and who God can and will be to them.

Second, the writer seeks an intimate experience with God in verse 4: "One thing I asked of the Lord, that will I seek after: to live in the house of the Lord, all the days of my life." Instead of losing their cool, the psalmist takes their stress and worry to the One who can handle it. And once there, they make some very specific prayer requests. It is critical that we take prayer seriously and be willing to share with God what truly troubles our hearts. Often, we cannot remain calm because we think we have no place to dump our fears and anxieties. Meanwhile, God is constantly waiting to remove them from us so that we can be free. May you always remember who your light is, who can save you, and to whom you belong.

POSITIVE VIBES

You'll do best by filling your minds
and meditating on things true, noble,
reputable, authentic, compelling,
gracious—the best, not the worst;
the beautiful, not the ugly; things to
praise, not things to curse.... Do that,
and God, who makes everything work
together, will work you into his most
excellent harmonies.
∽ PHILIPPIANS 4:8–9 (MSG)

In this passage, Paul is summing up a letter to some of his most beloved children in the faith. He had founded their church, was the first to preach the gospel there, and had taught them everything they knew. He shared a particularly good relationship with the church at Philippi, and it was his custom to keep in touch. But this time, he's writing to them from prison and wants to assure them that he is okay and also that his experience in jail has actually been good for the work of spreading the gospel (Philippians 1:12–14).

It's important to hear all of this context along with the present passage. Paul is in prison when he tells the Philippians the key to staying positive and how to protect their minds and hearts from negativity. It's a powerful thing to have lost your freedom but still be able to think clearly and give something helpful to others. These are real consequences he's facing, but somehow he has elevated his own mind above this matter, staying focused on his calling as an apostle to the Gentiles. In this way, Paul not only teaches the Philippians to stay positive in the midst of life's challenges, he also models it. He proves that it's possible to not let our circumstances cloud our perspective. We can remain committed to our mission despite the obstacles placed in our way. And how do we do that, exactly? Paul has a few ideas.

He instructs them to fill their minds with and meditate on good things—"the best, not the worst." What are you taking in? What are you reading, listening to, watching, or discussing? Does it uplift you? Encourage you? Is it rooted in truth and beauty? When we cultivate a mind full of these kinds of things, we cannot help but be inspired by them. Perhaps this is Paul's secret to staying positive despite being imprisoned. He is meditating on that which is real, gracious, and beautiful. Where does your mind go when you're facing challenges? What are you doing with your time? We would all do well to pour in positive things, nourishing our spirits in that which satisfies and lifts us up.

Another time it can be difficult to keep it positive is when we find ourselves in conflict with those around us. In committing ourselves to doing the work of faith and ministry, this may come up more than we like. Even in this very passage, Paul mentions such a conflict between two prominent women church leaders, Euodia and Syntyche (Philippians 4:2–3), and urges them to work past their differences.

Many are surprised to learn in these verses that women could hold prominent roles in the church at this time. That Paul specifically mentions these women and their disagreement, however, shows their importance as leaders, though we are not given the details of their roles. Neither are we told the content of the two women's disagreement, but we're all familiar with the ways different theological perspectives, leadership styles, or values can cause conflict, especially in the life of the church. We are encouraged in this instance not to ignore the conflict or become bogged down in any toxicity that arises but to address problems head-on and move past them. I suspect if both parties of a conflict would do as Paul is suggesting here—align their minds with what is good, authentic, compelling, noble, gracious, and true—they could do just that.

Please turn to the next page for a JOURNAL PROMPT. ⟫➔

JOURNAL PROMPT

How can or do you embrace positivity? In what ways can you protect your positivity, especially in the midst of difficulties? Try making a list of music, books, shows, or films that inspire you. Make a list of scriptures you wish to study. List all the people you know who uplift and encourage you. Next time you're facing something troublesome, revisit this list and begin to meditate on the points written out, and spend time with the people who can help you rise above them. Positive vibes only.

Do you have an unresolved conflict with a person of faith in your life? How have you responded to it? Does this passage encourage you to do something different?

ABIGAIL, CHIEF STRATEGIST

As she rode on the donkey and came
down under cover of the mountain,
David and his men came down toward
her; and she met them.
∽ 1 SAMUEL 25:20

Abigail was my kind of girl: a take-care-of-business, look-out-for-herself-and-her-community, do-what-she-has-to-do kind of woman. She didn't accept her impending fate as irreversible. Instead, she used what resources she had to turn a conflict into a conversation, violence into victory.

David was living in the wilderness, building his army and his influence. Though he was on the run from Saul, he had been anointed king, and it was only a matter of time before that became reality. He and his men needed sustenance, so he sent word to Nabal, a wealthy man, to request some. But Nabal, likely full of himself, refused to help—in direct conflict with Israel's practice of extending hospitality to all, especially the stranger. David, still in battle mode, prepared to ride out to kill Nabal and his men.

But Nabal's wife Abigail got wind of what was happening and jumped on her donkey to meet David as he approached, hoping that she could avert his plan to attack. Amazingly, she did. With a few words of wisdom, flattery, and humility, she got David to accept her gifts of food and kept him from going to kill her husband. You can almost feel her sigh of relief. She was probably shocked at what she was able to accomplish; perhaps she patted herself on the back and smiled at how she handled the matter all on her own despite her husband's cruelty and foolishness.

If we were to interview Abigail today and ask her what she learned from that ordeal, there are at least three lessons she might share. First, she might tell us not to underestimate ourselves. Abigail was a woman of means, but nonetheless living in a world controlled by men. She might not have thought it possible for her to make a difference. But whether she would be successful or not in stopping David's advance, she was willing to try. "Can't" wasn't in her vocabulary.

Second, sometimes you have to throw out the rule book. In her world, Abigail had no business interfering in the political affairs of her husband, but as Katharine Doob Sakenfeld points out in *Just Wives?: Stories of Power and Survival in the Old Testament and Today*, she made it her business and inserted herself in the conflict as an unlikely pacifist. Her willingness to step outside the lines drawn for her as a woman saved her life and many others'. When people's lives are on the line, that is no time to follow convention. Rather, embrace the spirit of what's right and advocate fully for it.

Finally, Abigail would tell us not to shy away from moments that require us to act. Some challenges don't give us time to think and reflect. They require bold action—*now*. We can't wait until it's convenient, until we're sure, until we're ready. There are moments when we must do something now in order to prevent disaster. We must learn to recognize these moments and be courageous enough to act on them.

Ultimately, Abigail emerges in this extended story as a wise woman, a brilliant strategist, and a leader who can be trusted to act when necessary. A forerunner of Esther, if you will, she takes a risk in order to save her household when her husband was negligent and foolish. She reminds us of what we can accomplish if we are willing to try. She used what she could for what she had to do. How can you apply Abigail-like actions in your life?

BEARING BATHSHEBA'S BURDEN: IT ISN'T YOUR FAULT

The woman conceived; and she sent
and told David, "I am pregnant."
∾ 2 SAMUEL 11:5

These words are for all the women who have long needed
to know that sexual assault and/or abuse wasn't their fault.
For those who were blamed for the harm done to them, who
carried the weight and the shame alone. For those whose
lives were forever altered by someone else's cruelty or care-
lessness. You've always known it was true in the pit of your
stomach, but you've also needed to hear it. If you've taken
the blame for an injury done to you and haven't been able
to shake yourself free from that emotional prison, Bathsheba
says it now. Lovingly looking upon you through the windows
of time, she whispers, "It isn't your fault." Not now, not then,
not ever. And if this isn't your story, it's the story of someone

you know, so listen along with those who bear this burden. May you share it with those who need to hear it.

Let Bathsheba recall her story:

How in the world did I get here? My life was good. I was happy. I was married to a good man. He was brave, honest, and loyal. It was spring; he was a military officer and was away fighting in routine battles (2 Samuel 11:1). I was at home minding my own business. I got up and had breakfast, bathed where I always did. But something different happened that day. Once I was dressed and ready to go about my day, some royal men came to my home demanding I go with them because the king had asked for me. It was odd. I'd never met him. What could he want? Had I done something wrong? Had my husband done something wrong? Or worse, was he dead? So many thoughts raced through my mind. But I went in obedience to our sovereign to see what the matter was.

Hours later, I woke up in his bed. I felt dizzy as I tried to come to terms with what had just happened. The king had called me to his palace for a rendezvous in the middle of the day. Me, a happily married woman! Now I was somehow guilty of having lain with someone other than my husband. I felt disgusting and dirty. All I wanted to do was take a bath, but apparently that's what had gotten me into this mess. He'd seen me bathing that morning and sent for me. He shouldn't have seen me, no one should have.

He wasn't even supposed to be home! He was supposed to be off fighting with his men—with my husband! I cried as I thought of my beloved. What would become of me now? Of him? Of us? Weeks later, my nightmares became my reality, and it sealed my fate. I was pregnant, and I knew it was David's (2 Samuel 11:4). In seconds, I had gone from a happy, faithful wife to an alleged adulteress.

Over the years, people have said the worst kinds of things about me, interpreting my story through the lens of lust and seduction on my part. But that's not how it happened. Here's the truth: I didn't ask for this. David sent for me, and he was the king. No one defies the king, certainly not the wife of a foreign military officer. I couldn't refuse, and if I had, it would have only gotten worse for me. He lusted after me, and he used his power to have me. I was stuck in a situation I did not create.

If you know the pain of landing in a place you had not planned, forced to do things you would never do, overpowered by those you could not protest against, know this: It wasn't your fault. The things they did belong to them, not you. The world can say what they want about you, but you know who you are and who you are not. Hold to the truth of your story and your character, and refuse to let others tell it. Tell it for yourself.

With love,

BATHSHEBA

THE PATH THAT PURPOSE OPENS

And this woman was a widow of about
eighty-four years, who did not depart
from the temple, but served God with
fastings and prayers night and day.
And coming in that instant she gave
thanks to the Lord, and spoke of Him
to all those who looked for redemption
in Jerusalem.
∾ LUKE 2:37–38 (NKJV)

Anna is one of those biblical characters we don't know much
about and barely even notice. Her story, if we can call it that,
is so brief that the entire thing is told in three verses. Thankfully for us, it's a power-packed three verses. We learn that
she was a widow of 84 and spent all her time worshipping
God in the temple. She wasn't some bored old lady; she was
a prophetess who stood in a long tradition of Israel's women
prophets, starting with Miriam. Anna had been through a lot,

having been married as a young woman and widowed only seven years later. Since that painful ordeal, she had spent the rest of her life working in the temple, having found her life's calling and passion as a prophetess.

Though there's not a ton of material on her, there are some important lessons we learn from Anna. First, she models for us that women—and all people, really—can experience fullness of life and purpose into old age. We live in a world that tends to discard people once they reach a certain age. Retirement can often feel like an imposed end to meaningful work, but Anna shows that there is much purpose and passion to be explored during our senior years. She was still serving her community as a prophetess at 84.

Anna also shows that there is life on the other side of death and tragedy. While we don't know how or why her husband died, we know that she only had him for seven years, and I'm sure that was painful. However, she discovered there was more to her than that experience. Grief can have a way of paralyzing us and tricking us into believing that the loss of our loved ones has to become our central focus, but that is not true. Look at what was waiting for Anna in the days after her loss: not only a meaningful life of service to her community but also an encounter with the Messiah. Because of that encounter, she was able to share the good news with all those who had been waiting for the promise of his coming. Imagine the joy this fostered inside her. It's another beautiful experience in her career as a prophetess and proves how important it is not to give up on life once tough times come.

If we keep waking up each day, that means God has something more for us to experience, something more to see and do. If we've lived to tell about something challenging, painful, or scary, then we know God has a purpose for us. Our job is to keep pursuing that purpose in order to discover what it is and fulfill it.

Please turn to the next page for a JOURNAL PROMPT. ⫸→

Write a journal entry about something awful that happened to you: a betrayal, breakup, job loss, loss of a loved one, etc. How did you experience grief during that time? How have you processed or worked through it—or not? What has your life been like on the other side of it? What good things have happened to you since?

Continue writing: How does Anna's story give you hope for a bright future despite the difficulty of your path? What does her story teach you? How do you identify with her or not? What lessons can you learn from her?

ELIZABETH, MARY, AND THE POWER OF COMMUNAL AFFIRMATION

"Now indeed, Elizabeth your relative
has also conceived a son in her old
age; and this is now the sixth month
for her who was called barren. For with
God nothing will be impossible."
∽ LUKE 1:36–37 (NKJV)

There really is something incredibly powerful about community when we allow it to open itself to us and embrace us. The exchange between Mary and Elizabeth recounted in Luke is a powerful example of what can happen when community works well. Mary had been a frightened unwed teenager who was told she was going to give birth to the Son of God. In her world, being unwed and pregnant was certainly a no-no, let alone being engaged but pregnant with someone else's child. But the angel Gabriel assured her everything would be fine.

God would cause her to conceive. And seeing her trying to understand how any of this could be happening, Gabriel reminded her that with God all things are possible. In fact, her older cousin Elizabeth, who had been barren and was now advanced in age, had conceived a child as well.

What a lot to process! Though the angel had assured her that God had chosen her for this special task, it still had to be overwhelming. Even good news can be stressful. She had to be uncertain about what lay ahead for her, but like the strong woman of faith she was, she accepted it all and took steps forward. But thank God she knew she didn't have to do so alone. When Gabriel told her that her cousin Elizabeth would also give birth, Mary probably felt better about her own circumstances because as soon as he said it, she put aside her confusion and agreed to the situation.

Have you ever had that happen? Was there a time when you were stressed about what lay ahead for you, but then someone shared a testimony about what God had already done in someone else's life and it encouraged you to keep moving forward? We should not look past these moments but stop to give God praise and thanks for them. Our stories of triumph never belong solely to us. Mary had not even spoken to Elizabeth herself, but what she heard was enough to give her courage, to believe she was capable of what was ahead. God had made it possible for Elizabeth, and God would make it possible for her.

In what ways have stories of other believers encouraged you on your journey? How have you opened yourself to allowing them to do so? Our faith is a shared, communal one, and at the heart of salvation is the question of reconciliation and our restored relationship with God. This means that relationship and community matter in the life of faith. It was never intended to be a private journey with God. Personal, sure, but communal at the same time. How do you allow the faith stories of others to strengthen and encourage you for the days ahead?

WEEK 51

THE BABE LEAPED

Then [Elizabeth] spoke out with a loud
voice and said, "... as soon as the voice
of your greeting sounded in my ears,
the babe leaped in my womb for joy.
Blessed is she who believed, for there
will be a fulfillment of those things
which were told her from the Lord."
 ∽ LUKE 1:42–45 (NKJV)

Once she accepted the blessing of being chosen by God to
give birth to the Messiah, Mary must've needed more encouragement. So she went to visit her cousin Elizabeth. Perhaps
hearing about Elizabeth's pregnancy was good enough to help
her say yes to what was happening, to willingly walk this path
of giving birth as a virgin and doing so within the very complicated circumstances of already being engaged to Joseph.
But actually living it out may have had her wondering how
she would or could do it. Whatever it was, something moved
Mary to take an extended trip to stay with her older cousin.

She must've known Elizabeth could help her through this exciting, scary, but incredibly blessed moment.

It is amazing how even when our lives are filled with hope, excitement, and anticipation for all things good, we still don't always know how to take it in, how to process it all, or how to embrace the goodness we've been given. We often need other people we know and love to show us the way. What do we make of our lives when they're finally filled with all the things we hoped for? Mary had only signed up for marriage; she had no idea this other blessing was waiting for her. Do you ever find yourself having a hard time taking in all the positive when it starts pouring your way? Does it feel overwhelming? Do you find you need to just sit and talk with someone who's been there?

I remember being terrified that God had called me to seminary. I knew I was supposed to go, but I wasn't sure what was ahead of me. I even tried to sabotage my going in a number of ways. But in fall of 2005, there I was in seminary. It wasn't until I attended the opening convocation and heard an incredible sermon that I finally settled down. The whole service, all I could hear and feel was: "You are in the right place. You are where you are supposed to be."

Look what happens when Mary reaches out for Elizabeth's support. As soon as Mary walks in, Elizabeth is blessed by her presence. The Spirit of God fills her up, and she knows that God has blessed Mary and called her to this important task. This feeling is so strong that even her own child feels it and leaps in her womb. What an incredible moment they share! Elizabeth wastes no time pouring out all the love and support that Mary needs. She confirms for Mary all that she had already been told and affirms Mary's choice to say yes to her calling.

When Elizabeth starts talking about how Mary is blessed among women and how she knows for certain God is going to keep every promise made to her, this has to overwhelm Mary with joy and give her the assurance she needs. She's not out of her mind. She made the right choice, and God is with her. Her community is affirming that. Everything is really going to be all right. In that moment, Mary can finally set free all the praise that she has stored up inside. Because out of that moment of love, support, and confirmation with Elizabeth, a deep and powerful praise bubbles up out of Mary, which is the subject of next week's devotion.

WEEK 52

AND MARY SAID ...

And Mary said,
"My soul magnifies the Lord,
and my spirit rejoices in God my Savior,
for he has looked with favor on the
lowliness of his servant.
Surely, from now on all generations will
call me blessed;
for the Mighty One has done great
things for me,
and holy is his name.
His mercy is for those who fear him
from generation to generation."
∾ LUKE 1:46–50

Known as one of the most famous songs in scripture, Mary's song of praise, the Magnificat, poured out of her in an overwhelming burst of gratitude. She knew she had been called to something great and had stepped out to go after it. But needing to understand it more, or perhaps reaching out for wisdom or affirmation, she went to see her older cousin. There's something about being embraced by our community that can inspire the deepest kind of praise. To know that someone believes in us, knows us, and can see what God is doing . . . it makes it real.

That kind of moment cannot help but crack open our hearts and let out all the emotion, the praise, the worship, the thanks. It confirms for us that God really is real, God really is good, there really is blessing for us, and the unimaginable is possible. It's like when you're trying to hold it all together, but then your mom looks at you and you burst into tears. There's something about being with those we love that won't let us hide what we're feeling.

Mary had a praise inside that she had to get out, and receiving those words of affirmation from Elizabeth made it so. There is something about feeling seen, known, and loved that makes us lose all pretense and release the truth of our pain, hopes, joy, and excitement. We can just be. Real love casts out fear. No longer fearful, Mary let out her deepest praise. And what did she say? *My soul is going to magnify the Lord, and my spirit will rejoice in my Savior. God considered little old me and has shown me favor.*

What favor of God in your life do you need to acknowledge? What great things has God done for you that you have yet to tell? What closed doors has God opened for you? Have you let others in your community affirm you in ways that will release the praise inside you? Or have you run away from them instead of toward them? How have you been listening to God and aligning yourself so that you can embody the spirit of Elizabeth and affirm the movement of God you see in others' lives? Who are you in this text: Mary, Elizabeth, or a combination of both?

Whatever you feel connected to in this exchange between Mary and Elizabeth, reach for the insight the story lends to you. Just like Mary, you have something beautiful to do and be in the world. No, you haven't been called to birth the Son of God, but God does have something that is strictly for each of us to do. The question is: Will we do it? And will we allow it to move us into a place of purpose and praise as it did for Mary? Or perhaps your calling is to help others accept and walk into theirs, like Elizabeth. Are you called to encourage, advise, and affirm? If so, then get to it! People are waiting on what you have to say. We all have something for which we are living, some purpose, some plan. Let's seek God about what that is and then ask for courage to pursue it. Amen.

Please turn to the next page for a GUIDED REFLECTION. ⫸→

GUIDED REFLECTION

Spend some time thinking about what you've been called to do. Do you know what it is? Have you been afraid to even ask? If you have been afraid, take comfort in the angel's words to Mary: "Do not be afraid, Mary, for you have found favor with God" (Luke 1:30). You are not alone. God is within you and will enable you to go after it. Moreover, God will send some Elizabeths your way to help you accept and embrace it. Do a little writing or some other creative activity that will give you space to think about what God is calling you to and how you can pursue it. The world is waiting on you, and you are totally capable of doing it.

GO FORTH WITH GOD

Sis, you did it! You committed yourself to journeying with some of the most intriguing women in the Bible. You listened to their stories, you learned from them, you allowed these ancient narratives into yours. Encountering the word of God and truly opening ourselves to what God is saying can often be challenging, because it asks us to change and grow. It demands openness, deeper faith, and greater trust in God. And you've boldly said yes to all that and stayed the course to the end. You should be proud that you had the courage to do this, to spend this kind of time with God and reach for more in your faith. Good for you. Good for all of us. This experience was always meant to shape us in new ways, grooming us for more maturity in Christ.

Through this experience, these women have taught us so much. Esther reminded us that we are all on a journey of becoming who God designed us to be and that, once we find ourselves in places of power, we should use that position to benefit others. Bathsheba powerfully reminded us that we are not responsible for the harm done to us. Ruth showed us how to save our own lives and refuse to be struck out by the curveballs life throws our way. The woman caught in adultery reminded us that our mistakes don't define us. Mary, sister of Martha, gave us permission to block out the world around us so that we can receive God's blessing and wisdom, while Martha reminded us to embrace who we are and what we do well without expecting others to be us or even be like us. Or perhaps Michal, Elizabeth, Mary, Sarah, Job's wife, or that sassy Syrophoenician unlocked some powerful life-changing truth for you.

Whatever this experience has been for you, I encourage you to give thanks and celebrate it. I mean it! Plan a special event with your friends or family that gives you space to name out loud what this journey revealed to you or your group. What have you learned from these women? How have your perceptions of them changed? How have your perceptions of yourself or other women you know changed? What will you take away from this experience that is most valuable to you? What new practices will you embrace? Write them down and then share them with loved ones and give thanks. In fact, that is your final assignment: Reflect on what you've learned on this journey, and plan some kind of event that allows you to share and celebrate it with others!

Thank you for allowing me to journey with you.

Blessings,
Ari

RESOURCES

Here are a few resources that will enrich your devotional experience, study of scripture, and understanding of women in the Bible.

Sabbath as Resistance: Saying No to the Culture of Now and *Praying the Psalms: Engaging Scripture and the Life of the Spirit* by Walter Brueggemann

Tweets for the Soul: When Life Falls Apart by Thema Bryant-Davis

Daily Destiny Readings: Inspirations for Your Life's Journey by T. D. Jakes

Boss Women Pray: 31 Prayers to Increase Your Success and Spirit by Kachelle Kelly

Successful Leaders of the Bible, Successful Moms of the Bible, and *Successful Women of the Bible* by Katara Washington Patton

God and the Rhetoric of Sexuality and *Texts of Terror: Literary-Feminist Readings of Biblical Narratives* by Phyllis Trible

Womanist Sass and Talk Back: Social (In)Justice, Inter-sectionality, and Biblical Interpretation and *I Found God In Me: A Womanist Biblical Hermeneutics Reader* by Mitzi J. Smith

Having a Mary Heart in a Martha World: Finding Intimacy with God in the Busyness of Life by Joanna Weaver

REFERENCES

Gafney, Wilda C. *Daughters of Miriam: Women Prophets in Ancient Israel*. Minneapolis, MN: Fortress Press, 2008.

———. *Womanist Midrash: A Reintroduction to the Women of the Torah and the Throne*. Louisville, KY: Westminster John Knox Press, 2017.

Newsom, Carol A., Sharon H. Ringe, and Jacqueline E. Lapsley, eds. *Women's Bible Commentary*. 3rd ed., rev. and updated. Louisville, KY: Westminster John Knox Press, 2012.

Sakenfeld, Katharine Doob. *Just Wives?: Stories of Power and Survival in the Old Testament and Today*. Louisville, KY: Westminster John Knox Press, 2003.

Smith, Mitzi J. *Womanist Sass and Talk Back: Social (In)Justice, Intersectionality, and Biblical Interpretation*. Eugene, OR: Cascade Books, 2018.

Solomon, Nancy D. *Impact!: What Every Woman Needs to Know to Go from Invisible to Invincible*. Hoboken, NJ: John Wiley & Sons, 2009.

Stewart, Anne W. "Eve and Her Interpreters." In *Women's Bible Commentary*, edited by Carol A. Newsom, Sharon H. Ringe, and Jacqueline E. Lapsley, 46–50. 3rd ed., rev. and updated. Louisville, KY: Westminster John Knox Press, 2012.

Trible, Phyllis. *God and the Rhetoric of Sexuality*. Philadelphia, PA: Fortress Press, 1978.

Von Rad, Gerhard. *Genesis: A Commentary*. rev. ed. Philadelphia, PA: Westminster Press, 1972.

Weems, Renita J. *Just A Sister Away: A Womanist Vision of Women's Relationships in the Bible*. Philadelphia, PA: Innisfree Press, 1988.

———. *What Matters Most: Ten Lessons in Living Passionately from the Song of Solomon*. New York, NY, and West Bloomfield, MI: Warner Books and Walk Worthy Press, 2004.

Williams, Delores S. *Sisters in the Wilderness: The Challenge of Womanist God-Talk*. Maryknoll, NY: Orbis Books, 2013.

INDEX

About the Author

Rev. Arionne Yvette Williams serves as associate chaplain at the University of Indianapolis's McCleary Chapel and is an ordained elder in the Missouri Conference of the AME Zion Church. The author of *Love Like I've Never Been Hurt: How to Heal from Heartbreak* and the creator of iSlay Bible Study, she also serves on the board of the Center for Interfaith Cooperation in Indianapolis. She holds a master of divinity degree from Garrett-Evangelical Theological Seminary and a certificate in youth and theology from Princeton Theological Seminary. Stay in touch with her on her website at ArionneYvette.com, on Instagram or Twitter at @MsArionneYvette, or on Facebook at Facebook.com/MsArionneYvette.

CPSIA information can be obtained
at www.ICGtesting.com
Printed in the USA
LVHW071315280120
644842LV00004B/2

9 781641 528115